DRIᖴT

"In a *dérive*, one or more persons during a certain period drop their relations, their work
and leisure activities, and all their other usual motives for movement and action, and let
themselves be drawn by the attractions of the terrain and the encounters they find there."
— Guy Debord, *Theory of the Dérive*, 1958.

The translation of *dérive* is *drift*.

STOCKHOLM

ADAM GOLDBERG
Editor in Chief

DANIELA VELASCO
Creative Director

ELYSSA GOLDBERG
Executive Editor

BONJWING LEE
Copy Editor

CONTRIBUTORS
Alex Kitain
Andrew Cole
Angela Almeida
Anna Brones
Annalisa Rosso
John Surico
Jonathan Shipley
Josefin Hååg
Lucas Oswald
Micha Van Dinther
Mikael Axelsson
Monica Takvam
Perry Fish
Rachel Eva Lim

WELCOME

Stockholm winters are dark, snowy, and cold. Massive scarves, thick socks, and charming holiday decorations can only stave off so much of the penetrating chill. When the sun sets around 2 pm, Swedes take shelter where it's warm: at home or in cafes, drinking cup after cup of freshly brewed coffee.

Comfort in Stockholm is synonymous with fika, the traditional Swedish coffee, pastry, and conversation break. Yet, just a decade ago, it was difficult to find hand-brewed coffee in the capital. Maybe you'd be welcomed into a grandparent's home with a cup from a percolator, but most likely you'd be sipping on machine-made drip.

It wasn't until Johan & Nystrom and Drop Coffee changed the way Stockholmers thought about coffee—by opening concept stores, founding customer education programs, and patiently and consistently serving excellent coffee they sourced and roasted themselves—that a specialty scene took off. Now, great coffee is all but expected in the Swedish capital. Nearly every Michelin-starred institution has a specialty coffee program run by a local roaster. Oaxen Krog even has its own blend.

Our fourth issue takes us through the Swedish capital, where coffee is brewed everywhere from avant-garde design firms to hotel boats docked in the misty harbor, by everyone from grandparents to tweens. Coffee is what brings Swedes together.

Adam Goldberg, Editor in Chief

Here Comes the Sun

PHOTO ESSAY Monica Takvam

Stockholm wakes up early. As I wander the city at the crack of dawn, people emerge—quietly, sleepily—from neighboring apartment buildings in search of caffeine. It's still dark.

Frederik is walking his dog, Sammi, before work. Fred no longer works near Chokladkoppen, his favorite cafe in the city, but he'll take his coffee black from a nearby cafe anyway. He's giving a presentation today, and needs his first coffee of the day to set him up for success.

I meet Mikel at a bus stop. We're huddled beneath a curved glass roof we were using as makeshift shelter from the rain. Mikel is smoking a cigarette and carrying a thermos. He's looking forward to the cappuccino he'll brew at the office on the floor above the one that houses his desk.

Two contractors outside a block of flats at 7 am turned up for a job only to find they are locked out and have to wait for the keys. Until those keys arrive, the contractors will pause for coffee. Black with one sugar, no milk—it's the first cup of the day.

The streets are blue. The whole city is blue. The sun seems tired, almost as if it's debating whether to call in sick and spend all day beneath the covers. It takes longer to rise in Stockholm than the sun I'm used to in London. When the city is blanketed with this soft, periwinkle blue, only carpenters and bakers seem to be wake.

Apparently, babies are too. Ekaterina waits for her daughter Elsa to fall asleep in the pram. Elsa has irregular sleeping hours: 5 am to 8 am, precisely when her mother wants to keep her eyes shut. The cafe where I find them is halfway between Ekaterina's flat and the daycare where Elsa will spend the day.

Though so many people are out, it's surprisingly quiet. Cars are careful not to honk or screech. Trains seemingly sneak out from their stations. The city must only turn up the volume once the sunlight casts pink light onto the orderly buildings.

At Drop Coffee, Honest Al wakes up. He runs the barber shop across the road, and before he can attend to dozens of beards, he needs a cup of coffee and a quick hello from Erik, a barista.

After days of dark, heavy rain, the sun is on its way.

Drop Coffee is Sara's cafe of choice. As she reaches for yet another cup, she warns me that she drinks close to 15 cups per day. Small ones, she reassures. I'm clearly concerned. She adds that she doesn't smoke, and she doesn't use snus [Swedish tobacco powder]. Coffee is her drug. I'm wide-eyed. She laughs and takes another sip.

The city is now orange. The sun is up. •

Fika

WORDS Anna Brones
PHOTOGRAPHS Daniela Velasco

It's hard to go a day in Sweden without hearing someone say "fika." Used as both a verb and a noun, fika—pronounced FEE-KAH—is the Swedish word for coffee break. But it's not a generic catchall term; it describes an integral part of Swedish culture that dates back centuries. It's the word written on cafe blackboards, mandated in offices, the one that binds friends and families to one another.

Fika is essentially synonymous with coffee, although tea can count as well. It involves a sweet treat, most frequently cinnamon and cardamom buns—or, depending on the occasion, salty and briny open-faced sandwiches too.

What's distinctly Swedish isn't that Swedes are drinking coffee or eating herring on rye. It's how they are doing it.

The word fika was first recorded in 1913: an inversion of the two syllables in kaffe, the Swedish word for coffee. But the custom predates the term, to the late 1800s and early 1900s, when coffee, for the first time, became an everyday product consumed by the general public. Like much of Europe, coffee was initially available as a luxury product in Sweden, before slowly trickling down to the masses, where it earned its place as the country's national drink.

Coffeehouses of the 1700s were predecessors to modern cafes, and were intended as places visitors could come for a cup of coffee. But it wasn't until the 1800s that Sweden welcomed its first *konditori*, a combination upscale coffeehouse and patisserie that, even today, is steeped in the city's coffee culture. Going to a posh konditori was a special event, particularly for city dwellers who would indulge in a popular Sunday family tradition of a cup of coffee and a slice of cake or delicate pastry. In many Swedish cities, iconic and upscale konditori are still around today, like Ofvandahls in Uppsala, which dates to the 1800s, and Stockholm's Vete-Katten, which was founded in 1928.

The social aspect of fika continued well into the 1900s, when the expression *kyrkkaffe* became popularized. "Church coffee," as it was translated literally, signified a social gathering held after church service, when coffee, tea, small sandwiches, and cakes were set out for anyone who wanted to stay and socialize.

Even those who weren't churchgoers recognized coffee as a social glue. In the mid-1900s, kafferep, formal coffee gatherings hosted in people's homes, became the event du jour. They always came with coffee and a specific assortment of treats, including small cookies, buns, and cakes, and were hosted for everything from birthday parties to funerals. Sweet breads and cakes served at these gatherings earned the name kaffebröd, or coffee bread.

Today, fika is a much more casual affair, as simple as a low-key cup of coffee and a cookie. Yet its social importance has never wavered. Coffee is to the Swedes what wine is to the French. As Joanna Alm of Drop Coffee Roasters puts it: "No matter the occasion, we're drinking coffee."

For Swedes, fika is a custom that bridges age, gender, and race; you are just as likely to get together over coffee with your grandmother as you are with your colleagues. It brings people together in a way that nothing else does; it is an excuse to take a break from the modern, hectic world. It's not something you push off until a spot in your calendar opens up later in the week.

In Swedish workplaces, mornings and afternoons have built-in fika breaks, time set aside so you can step away from your computer and interact with coworkers. Outside of the office, fika can be as low-maintenance as a last-minute coffee with a friend, or it can be the perfect excuse to host an elaborate party.

In Swedish, "Ska vi fika?" ("Shall we fika?") carries far more social importance than the only corresponding English phrase "Do you want to grab a cup of coffee?" It's simpler, but it manages to say more. It isn't just about coffee, and Swedes know that. Instead, if you're asking to fika, you're really saying, "Let's take a break. Let's slow down, catch up, and enjoy a moment together."

Fika is the thread that weaves Swedish social customs together, and it's the ultimate nod to the idea of slow living. In our fast-paced world, where we are constantly on deadline or planning our schedules around meetings and events, we crave opportunities to slow down. Swedes actually embrace those opportunities.

Carving out time for a break like that has global appeal. It's why the philosophy behind fika has been exported all over the globe, from FIKA, a chain in New York, to fika-themed cafes in London, Seoul, and Sydney.

Fika demands that we create space in our lives for a break. It discourages getting a cup of coffee to go and drinking it in solitude in front of a computer. Fika is about slowing down, getting together with friends, and spending a moment completely present in the company at hand. As any Swede will tell you, life without fika is unthinkable. •

But First, Pastries

PHOTO ESSAY Adam Goldberg and Daniela Velasco

Dense balls of dark chocolate dredged in coconut flakes. Intricately braided cinnamon buns laced with fragrant cardamom and dotted with chunky pearl sugar. Spongy rye bread propping up hefty layers of chilled fish. A pastry for a meeting with long-lost friends, another for family gatherings, and another still for students powering through brutal all-nighters. Bites are bookended by sips of coffee served black. It's all in a day's fika, where the pastries that accompany the traditional coffee break are as vibrant and varied as the conversation.

Chokladboll (Chocolate Ball)

Prinsesstårta (Princess Cake)

Surdegsbröd (Sourdough)

Kardemummabulle (Cardamom Roll)

Kanelbulle (Cinnamon Roll)

Chokladbiskvi (Chocolate Biscuit)

Spatial Relations

WORDS Rachel Eva Lim
PHOTOGRAPHS Daniela Velasco

"You can't serve crappy coffee in a beautifully designed masterpiece, and you can't serve high quality coffee in a place with shitty design." Johan Damgaard lives and breathes this philosophy at Johan & Nyström, the cafe he co-founded in Stockholm's hip Södermalm neighborhood in 2004. "Great coffee in a perfectly designed environment is like heaven."

While coffee is still at the core of his business, Damgaard and other Stockholm coffee shop owners acknowledge the effect that design has on quality of life. Indeed, they've harnessed key Swedish design principles to provide patrons with the best possible overall experience: principles such as prioritizing functionality over mere aesthetic appeal, engaging customers on an emotional level, incorporating natural materials, and focusing just as much on the little design flourishes as the larger structural construction processes.

The initial blueprints for Johan & Nyström's concept store adhered to a "function is God" approach. The cafe's architecture had to communicate its purpose and also be a pleasant place to inhabit. The layout had to allow for an easy flow of movement. The counter had to house the world's first integrated AeroPress bar. And the interior had to regulate the amount of light entering the premises—crucial considering dark and dreary Swedish winters that give way to long hours of daylight during the few summer months.

"We thought about how different materials reflect light and how and where the sunlight entered the space," Damgaard says. "We placed lighter materials in the coffee shop's dark spots, and darker objects where the warm beams of sunlight could reach them." Balancing the degree of light throughout the cafe ensures a uniformly lit environment, which prevents customers from having to settle for a dingy back-corner table when they can't snag a seat by the window. Coupled with bright walls that reflect the light instead of engulfing it, as well as large windows, Damgaard has created an ideal spot for patrons to soak up as much mood-boosting vitamin D as possible.

Equally important to determining Johan & Nyström's design was a desire to facilitate an engaging customer experience. This is a concept store, where Johan & Nyström conducts a range of amateur and professional barista classes, is as much of an education and training center as it is a cafe.

"We wanted to put on a show for the customers and allow them to see how we prepare their drinks, so we tried to strip the space of all physical barriers and obstacles," Damgaard says. To do this, he installed an open bar seating area where customers can interact with baristas and watch their coffee being made. Damgaard says that giving patrons this inside look into the coffee-making process is like inviting them into his kitchen, the heart of his home. Watching expert baristas brew coffee can be hypnotic. And doing away with traditional partitions fosters a sense of intimacy and transparency, allowing cafe visitors to feel like they're part of the community. "When we highlight these altars where we perform our brewing and cupping rituals, the customers witness our dedication to our craft and want to come back."

Swedish design also makes ample use of natural materials. These organic elements, such as wood, stone, cork, and marble, combine with ruthless editing to create trademark Swedish style: minimalist, simple, clean, and cozy. Natural materials recreate the feeling of being outdoors and—combined with large insulated windows and neutral walls—amplify a space, preventing it from feeling too cramped or claustrophobic. For Stockholm locals, who rarely spend extended periods of time outside in the winter, this is of the utmost importance.

"Swedes have a long history of working with natural materials, and we make it a priority to use high-quality equipment and really take the time to build things properly," says Joanna Alm, CEO and head roaster of Drop Coffee Roasters near Stockholm's Mariatorget. Different shades and textures of wood dominate Drop Coffee's spacious premises—from expansive window frames and exterior bench seating to wooden chairs and countertops where baristas expertly assemble espresso drinks. Inside, Drop Coffee harnesses warm light fixtures, wood pallet furnishings, concrete flooring, as well as plush sofas and armchairs from Nordic Care, to create an environment that is "more bohemian than clinical," as Alm describes it, making it an inviting spot to linger over a cup of coffee.

Other than its aesthetic appeal, using natural materials ensures the interior has a certain durability and enduring quality. It buffers against the very real possibility that the staff will get tired of looking at it day in and day out, and delays redecorating. "We didn't want to make one of those prestigious, expensive, and famous designer places that quickly go out of style," Damgaard says of why he integrated organic elements, such as wood, metal, and various stones. "The plan was to build an honest, timeless space that could have been there for the past 10 years and continue to exist without getting boring for another 10 years."

Designing a coffee shop that would stand the test of time was also the aim of Café Pascal owner Arman Seropian. When collaborating with his brother to construct the Vasastan cafe from scratch, Seropian devised a visual identity that mirrored the top-quality and craftsmanship of their coffee. "We wanted it to feel timeless and give the impression that it's existed for the past five decades, but we also wanted a space that we'd be happy to work in every single day," he says. Café Pascal's high ceilings give way to exposed brick walls and a mixture of wood and marble furniture, while the main countertop injects a splash of light teal into the otherwise monochromatic space. Seropian's favorite items are the industrial lights that date back to the early 1900s and "come from old Swedish factories that don't exist any longer." Paired with the cafe's more modern furnishings, they create the classic, timeless effect that Seropian first envisioned.

The smaller objects are equally important and deliberately considered. It's a shop owner's nightmare for a customer's otherwise flawless experience to be tainted by something as minor as a rusty serving spoon, a chipped mug, or a menu that disintegrates while perusing its worn-out pages.

It's not easy to prize functionality and simplicity while channeling the comforts one could just find at home. But Stockholm's cafes are keen on trying. Alm likes customers to feel as if they're relaxing in their own living rooms. Seropian does too: "Many people regard coffee shops as their second home, which makes us, as owners, want to create something special. Cafes and people have existed together for centuries."

For Damgaard, it's impossible to separate the actual coffee beverage from the surroundings in which it's consumed. "Fika allows you to pause time, enjoy a cup of coffee, and reflect on the people and the environment that surround you," he says. "Great coffee coupled with great interior design is like therapy—except way less stressful and significantly cheaper." •

Where To Find Me

WORDS Perry Fish
PHOTOGRAPHS Daniela Velasco

Erik Pettersson is a regular. Every morning, on his way to work, he walks his daily route down Nortullsgatan toward busy Odenplan, and pops into Café Pascal. The spacious cafe has white walls, exposed brick, blonde wood, hints of teal, and so much light—courtesy of pendant and swing-arm lamps as well as massive windows—that, even in winter, Café Pascal feels like a brief sojourn to a sunny isle. He takes a moment to chat with whoever is behind the counter and gets the lowdown on what happened at the cafe since his last visit. He waves hello to any other regulars he's met before, and orders a V60 brew—the usual. Sometimes, he even visits twice a day, and on those occasions, he orders the porchetta sandwich for lunch. On each day he returns, he's proud to have made this cafe his own.

Pettersson, who used to work at a specialty coffee roaster, stumbled upon Café Pascal on the first day it opened in 2013. Hosep, Arman, and Jannet Seropian, siblings and owners of the cafe, had been welcoming customers for only a few hours. Pettersson doesn't remember what he ordered, but he remembers overhearing a conversation between the owners and close friends and family who stopped by to wish them good luck. What stuck with him was the warmth with which loved ones congratulated the team, how excellent that first cup of coffee there was, and how forthcoming and warm Hosep was when Pettersson pried about details.

Three years later, after Café Pascal has earned a Gulddraken—an annual award presented to the best restaurants, bars, and cafes in Stockholm by *Dagens Nyheters*, Sweden's largest daily newspaper—Pettersson is still a devoted customer. He loves the coffee, of course, but the friendly staff, other loyal patrons, and good vibes of the place keep him coming back day after day. •

Acquired Taste

INTERVIEW AND PHOTOGRAPHS
Adam Goldberg and Daniela Velasco

It's hard to overlook Jesper Bood. The blonde Swede, who stands at over six feet tall, with a thick beard and a deep voice, speaks with conviction and commands attention. He started his career as a barista in Australia almost a decade ago, just as third wave coffee was gaining momentum in cities all over the world. But it wasn't until he moved to Sweden in 2010 to work with a roaster called da Matteo out of Gothenburg that he hit his stride as a meticulous barista and earned the de facto role of Stockholm coffee historian. Since then, he has consulted at small retail shops and wholesale roasters, as well as for restaurant coffee programs committed to leaving Nespresso pods behind. Inside the Dome of Visions, a geodesic dome in central Stockholm where Bood had a coffee bar, he poured us cups and let us in on a few secrets about how the growing specialty coffee scene is shaking out in Stockholm—and why it may never grow to be as big as the scene in some of the world's other coffee capitals.

-

What's happening in Stockholm coffee right now?
People who were previously employed by the early players have now started to open places of their own with new, interesting concepts. You have, for instance, a place called Tous Les Jours run by a guy who used to be at Science Cafe. The other thing over the last couple of years is that successful cafes making great coffee are now also making great food in addition to baked goods such as cinnamon rolls and traditional Swedish pastries. The overall quality of cafes has risen. You can't do great coffee and serve bad soup anymore. Everything has to be great.

What about the other way around? What about the restaurants that have typically had bad coffee?
Too many Michelin-starred restaurants still use Nescafé or Nespresso, but some of the major players are showing an increased interest in coffee. In Gothenburg, da Matteo works with one or two of the starred restaurants. In Stockholm, it's Drop Coffee or Johan & Nyström. Where there is a focus on flavors and fresh produce overall, there should also be a focus on coffee. I think more restaurants will begin to follow suit.

What's it like to open a small business here?
There is a lot of red tape and intense regulation. But once you open up a shop and take care of potential errors, it's quite easy to do another shop. Actually, the cost of hiring a staff is the biggest problem with opening any business in Stockholm. Wages in Sweden are very, very high compared to other countries in Europe. That's the major issue for a lot of people.

Who are the big roasters right now in Stockholm?
Johan & Nyström is the original player and the biggest on an international scale; it started up in 2005. Drop Coffee, located across the street from Johan & Nyström, is their biggest competition. Drop has always been a competitive place in general: The baristas participate in coffee competitions. Being hungry for knowledge has really paid off for them. Johanna Alm is one of the owners now, and she placed second in the World Coffee Roasting Championship. That's earned them a lot of attention. We still need someone to go in and change the commodity clients into specialty.

What's the hesitation?
If you look at the way coffee quality is scored, specialty coffee receives a score of around 80 plus. Commodity coffee in Sweden is around 50 or 60, even though in Germany or other European countries, it's only 30 or 40. Comparatively, Swedish commodity coffee is quite good.

What do you mean?
We have a few problems with the way people are accustomed to drinking coffee in Sweden. For one, dark roasts are more popular here, but for strange reasons. Roasting coffee dark originates in the south of Sweden where the water is much harder. But roasting coffee dark when you're in that part of the country actually results in pleasant flavors. The water here in Stockholm is much lighter, so dark roasted coffee tastes worse. Because people have become so accustomed to dark roasts, they don't see a problem with it. It's why the idea of "strong" or "bold" coffee has been mistakenly conflated with "good coffee" here.

Has that made it harder for specialty coffee to take off in Stockholm?
Another problem has to do with Swedish coffee culture, more generally. Coffee has always been included with the price of meals in Sweden. If you purchased lunch somewhere, coffee came with free refills. Then there is free coffee in every workplace. Basically, people in Stockholm are used to drinking a lot of coffee for free.

How can you justify charging people more for coffee then?
Well, you put it in an espresso machine, put a tie on the guy making the cup, and pour milk in it. You tell customers that this guy makes coffee for a living, and that he's very skilled and well-educated. You have to pay him money though. All of a sudden, you can't just charge five kronor; you have to charge 25 kronor for a latte, which makes sense to Swedish people. Then, years later, you take away the latte with the milk, and you serve brewed coffee at that same premium. It's a challenge to make people understand that specialty coffee isn't what they're used to, even if it looks the same visually—and prices reflect that.

How do people react?
People don't necessarily get that expensive brewed coffee is a symbol that the quality of coffee, and the quality of the work put into it, has increased. And when cafes charge 20 or even 50 kronor for a specific coffee where they've cultivated relationships with a reclusive grower, the customer just asks, "Well, I want a regular coffee. Can I get that?"

Do customers in Stockholm tend to stay at the coffee shops, or take it to go?
The chains here have created demand for takeaway coffee in recent years. But I still think the fika tradition anchors our culture and makes a lot of people want to stay and linger over coffee. You finish your coffee within the walls, basically—unless you work in an office.

What does this mean for the Stockholm coffee scene at large?
It's a big problem for local coffee shops in residential areas. People don't buy their coffee near their homes when they are on their way to work. They buy it as close to their workplace as possible, to maintain a little bit of freedom before heading into a workday. Every sip of coffee reminds them, "I'm not fully at the office yet. I'm still out here, doing my own thing." Takeaway coffee here is more like the new cigarette in Stockholm.

In many places in the world, the morning is the busiest part of the day at a cafe, because it coincides with rush hour. Is it the same in Stockholm or is there a fika rush?
The way people are drinking coffee in Stockholm is changing. Espresso has always targeted commuters, and a lot of the quality coffee shops serve espresso. So their rush hour is probably bigger than rush hour at a cafe that only serves brewed coffee. We did brewed coffee at the Dome, so we got a second rush just after lunch when people wanted to sit for a coffee, meet friends, or fika on parental leave. What the pub is to Londoners, the coffee house is to people in Stockholm: a meeting point. •

The Queen of Spices

WORDS Jonathan Shipley
PHOTOGRAPHS Adam Goldberg and Daniela Velasco

In India, where it's native to the mountain ranges of Kerala, it's called elaichi, illaichi, or elaychi. A shade-loving perennial with long, lance-like green leaves that grow as much as three- to six-feet-tall, cardamom, as we refer to it in English, flourishes in the humid rainforests of southwest India. Called "the queen of spices" there, cardamom thrives in shady monsoon forests enveloped in soft morning mists along the rugged hillsides. Its harvest season brings white blossoms streaked with purple, resembling small orchids, which are as beautiful as they are fragrant.

Over 4,500 miles away, in Stockholm, kardemumma is everywhere, an unavoidable staple of Swedish fika.

The earliest mention of cardamom is written in Ebers Papyrus, which dates to 1500 BC, and chronicles the Egyptian use of the spice in medicines, teeth-cleaning, embalming, and in other ritualistic practices. And cardamom first made it to the Western world as early as the 4th century BC, according to ancient Greek trade texts. Travelers brought the spice along for its medicinal value—and because the exotic spices of India could be sold at a premium in the west.

By the 1st century CE, Rome was importing large amounts of cardamom. Hippolos and Vultumus, propelled by powerful monsoon winds, were able to make voyages between Europe and India. As trade routes opened, Phoenicians, Greeks, and Romans brought an abundance of spices back for medicinal purposes and cooking. Sweet and invigorating, cardamom quickly became one of the most popular Asian spices in Roman cuisine.

Some date its presence in Scandinavia further back to the Vikings who, thousands of years ago, supposedly discovered cardamom while exploring Constantinople. Legend has it that, by the time the green cardamom pods survived the long voyages overseas from the east, they appeared whiter and tasted milder due to extended exposure to air, salt, and sun. Northern Europeans developed a taste for the peculiar spice—which tastes of herbs and citrus and pairs best with warming spices such as cinnamon and nutmeg—incorporating it into pastries, meatballs, and traditional mulled wine (glögg).

Cardamom was first mentioned in Scandinavian cookbooks in the 1300s when various recipes recommended it as a palliative. Due to its rarity and cost, for years cardamom was only indulged by Sweden's upper class. One age-old myth claims it even helped kill a king. On Fat Tuesday, 1771, after King Adolf Fredrik ate 14 servings of his favorite dessert–htevagg–a variation of semla served with warm milk and sprinkled with cinnamon, he died. While no one knows the precise cause of his untimely death, as the story goes, he died of gluttony (and extreme indigestion). As any Swede will tell you, one semla is never enough.

Centuries later, cardamom has become one of the most common flavors in any Swedish meal—especially if it's fika. "For Swedes, cardamom buns take you back to your childhood," says Birgitta Palmer, who works for the Stockholm Visitor's Board. "Reminders of having a freshly baked bun in the kitchen at your grandma's to accompany fika, or coming home from school and retrieving a bun from the lady next door. Nothing smells better than coming home to someone making freshly baked cardamom buns." Per ounce, cardamom is still one of the most expensive spices on earth. Only saffron and vanilla cost more by weight.

Today, Guatemala is the world's biggest producer and exporter of cardamom, followed by India and Sri Lanka. Cultivation of cardamom was introduced to Guatemala before World War I by a German coffee planter, Oscar Majus Kloeffer. By 1980, Guatemala surpassed India in worldwide production. The world's biggest consumers today are in Saudi Arabia and Kuwait, where people use it extensively to enhance the flavors of their coffee. The European Union imports 1,200 tons of cardamom annually—and the leading EU consumer of cardamom is Sweden, followed by Finland and Germany.

Fika culture, and the style of Swedish baking associated with it, has spread globally. In Chicago, Illinois, Eliza Williamson, general manager of Swedish Bakery, runs one of the few traditional Swedish bakeries in America. Williamson, who previously owned a bakeshop in Cincinnati, specializes in Swedish baked goods and tries to bring a taste of fika to Americans. Cardamom coffee cake, made from a cardamom dough filled with cinnamon and almonds, is her specialty. And the spice is essential to getting the Swedish flavor profile just right. "Enjoying cardamom toast while drinking coffee with my family during the holidays is just about perfect," she says, noting that one of her greatest joys at Swedish Bakery is shipping products to homesick Swedes throughout the United States. "Cardamom has a deeply rooted history in Swedish baking and fika," Williamson says. "We're continuing that tradition here in Chicago."

Back in Stockholm, the sun has barely risen over the city-of-islands, but the city's bakers are hard at work. At Vete-Katten, a traditional konditori, or patisserie, along the lively Kungsgatan that has been around since the 1920s, Johan Sandelin is opening up shop. "My father used to be a chef," he tells me, "so on weekends we used to bake cinnamon rolls as a way to bond." After years of being a pastry chef, his favorite is still semla, the irresistible Swedish cardamom bun filled with almond paste and freshly whipped cream, traditionally served during Lent. Now, like bakers all over the city, he makes cardamom buns every morning so that, hours later, when the rest of Stockholm wakes, finding them is as easy as stopping for fika at one of the many coffeehouses and bakeries in the city. •

Separating the Coffee from the Chaff

WORDS Alex Kitain
PHOTOGRAPHS Adam Goldberg

Every day, when I close my tasting bar in Amsterdam, I carry bag after bag of waste to the garbage cans that line the street outside. It's not like the thought never occurred to me that I could do something better with my used coffee grounds than disposing of them in large black plastic bags. Once, I made a nice coconut oil coffee scrub with it. But, as an everyday practice, it's unsustainable.

In Stockholm, Martin Berg of the Michelin two-starred restaurant Mathias Dahlgren may have found a solution for at least one component of the massive quantities of waste coffee shops discard. After visiting Drop Coffee's roaster Joanna Alm one day to check on a custom coffee roast he had ordered for his restaurant, Berg had one of those Eureka moments. "Joanna was walking me through the coffee roasting process when I noticed delicate, golden flakes dancing around in the air. I asked her what they were, and she said they are called 'chaff,' and are a byproduct of coffee roasting. She also said they're edible. I was like: 'You don't say?'"

Chaff is the term used to describe the husks of the coffee bean that come off during the roasting process; they're normally collected on a tray or in a tank. Although incredibly lightweight, chaff is expansive in volume. To give you an idea: a regular retail bag for 250 grams of coffee could be filled to the brim with chaff and weigh only 35 grams. In most instances, chaff is disposed, but in the case of Drop Coffee, it just took someone like Berg to come in with a fresh pair of eyes to find a better use for it.

That day at the Drop roastery, Berg grabbed a handful of the fluffy flakes, with their delicate golden color, and put them into his mouth. "The taste was bitter, but also sweet, not unlike the sensation you get from 70 percent pure cacao chocolate bars. At the same time, it instantly turned to mush in my mouth, like eating a spoonful of flour. It got me thinking," Berg said.

In a country like Sweden, which has a proud baking heritage, and easy access to organic and heirloom grains, coming across a new baking ingredient is disproportionately exciting. Berg's handful of chaff inspired him to ask Alm for a full bag of the stuff. He brought it to Mathias Dahlgren's bakery, The Green Rabbit, and sat down with the pastry chefs to sell them on the potential value of getting this overlooked byproduct into the kitchen.

What they came up with, after some experimentation, were new chocolate cakes and rye breads, in which chaff replaced some of the flour. Berg explained, "On its own, chaff doesn't have a unique flavor to identify it outright, but it works great in combination with other things. Chaff is not self-raising, but it is gluten-free and adds texture that's both subtle and distinctive."

It didn't take much convincing for me to want to get my hands on some of the stuff myself. I called my friend Jeremy Greene, head roaster at Lot Sixty One Coffee Roasters in Amsterdam. He promised to save me a bag of chaff from his next production round. "What do you want this for?" he asked. I told him the truth: "I'm not exactly sure, actually. I think it's some new kind of superfood and I want to try it." He looked at me quizzically for about four seconds too long—then burst out laughing and shooed me away so he could concentrate on his work.

Indeed, calling chaff a superfood isn't totally off the mark. It is packed with caffeine and minerals that make it an ideal organic fertilizer for plants and compost. During my call with Joanna, she told me that she'd been using chaff in her gardening for years, and swore that her tomato, rhubarb, and pumpkin plants thrived because of it. She shrugged, "They just come out a lot juicier and with more flavor with the chaff, you know?"

Greene delivered on the chaff. I promised him full details. I returned home with a bag and took a moment to examine it. If you told me it was finely sliced oats for making porridge, I wouldn't have questioned it. With it, I did what anyone would do: I proceeded to stuff my mouth with a heaping handful. Sure enough, as Berg previously described, the chaff dissolved on my tongue like tiny snowflakes, coating my tongue with a layer of sticky goo.

The taste was negligible and I struggled to clearly identify it as either bitter or sweet. Its volume-to-weight ratio is perplexing, to say the least. How do you package and sell something that barely has any weight but needs to be sized out in variable quantities?

Drop Coffee figured it out. The roasting operation is already sharing its chaff with Berg's previous employer, Rosendals Trädgård, an organic farm in the heart of the Swedish capital that grows its own fruit and vegetables, which are served at its popular cafe, and sold at its shop. In recent months, the farmers there have been using chaff as a fertilizer for the farm's tomatoes and cucumbers.

"In California, many organic farms are already using chaff in the production process because they recognized early on that its nutritional value can give a natural boost to the soil," Berg explained. "Here in Sweden, we're still at the very early stages of experimenting with it, but so far the results have been very promising."

Currently, Drop Coffee serves pastries and cakes from The Green Rabbit that contain its own chaff. They've been well-received so far, said Berg. Alm would still like to see more chaff made available for purchase. "I would really love if our guests could take it home and use it for gardening. It would allow us to paint a more complete picture of coffee as a natural product and showcase the various elements that come out of coffee production." The dream? A standard order—a macchiato and a kanelbullar—punctuated with an eager request for a kilo of chaff, a byproduct previously discarded, bag after bag, in bins outside of coffee shops worldwide, now prized for merits beyond mere self-satisfaction. ∎

To Have and To Hold

WORDS Anna Brones
PHOTOGRAPHS Daniela Velasco

At the age of 101, my Swedish grandmother still drinks coffee out of her porcelain cups. They are elegant—white porcelain painted with flowers—and they date to years long before I was born.

According to a study published in the *Journal of Sensory Studies* in 2013, different colored cups affect the perceived flavor of beverages. That is, the vessel from which we drink has as much of an influence on our perception of taste as what we are actually drinking. We experience a cup of coffee differently if it's in an orange mug versus a white mug, or if it's served in ceramic versus porcelain.

Now think of your ideal coffee mug. It feels a certain way when it touches your lips. Your fingers clasp around the handle for a certain comfortable fit. Certain ceramic or porcelain keeps your coffee at just the right temperature for just the right amount of time. Whatever you're serving, whoever you're drinking it with, the ideal cup can heighten the experience.

In Sweden, coffee cups are an art form, their function matched with their aesthetic. They are prized possessions among coffee lovers in the country. Swedish cupboards contain an array of coffee cups, ranging from those used everyday to ones reserved for special occasions, like birthdays, visits from friends we haven't seen in years, or more formal get-togethers. Given that coffee is a staple of Swedish culture, it's no surprise that Swedish drinking vessels have become a symbol of Swedish design and tradition.

Swedish design is marked by simplicity, functionality, and beauty, which come together harmoniously in products ranging from highly conceptual to mundane. The coffee cup is no exception. "We Swedes are often associated with 'clean' design," says Christina Strandberg, chief executive at Gustavsbergs Porslinsfabrik, the renowned Swedish porcelain factory founded in 1825. Patterning is allowed but it must be simple and sophisticated, and without excessive decoration or gold leaf.

Porcelain sets, in particular, are prized family possessions, often handed down through the generations. A set may contain a coffee cup, an accompanying saucer, a pitcher for cream, a bowl for sugar, and a coffee pot.

Whenever someone comes to visit, the sets come out: It's an essential part of gathering in a home over coffee and snacks. For generations, Swedes have grown up with this ritual. The use of the fine china whenever company is over imbues ordinary company with a sense of dignity, a nod to the importance of ritual and tradition.

But the younger generation, which associates porcelain with the fussiness of their grandparents, aren't observing this custom as closely. Though, in recent years, the idea of slow-living has reemerged as a way of defraying the chaos of the everyday, plugged-in life of the 21st century.

That nostalgia can be seen in the recent obsession Swedes, and foreigners hoping to emulate a Scandinavian way of life, have for classic vintage porcelain designs. Take the mid-1950s patterns designed by Stig Lindberg for Gustavsberg Porslinsfabrick as an example. Lindberg's bold colors, including cobalt blue and emerald green; sleek shapes; and repeating patterns represented a fresh approach to porcelain at the time. And, while decades old, they have managed to age well. In fact, they've become so popular among younger generation in recent years that they're a constant fixture on the shelves at department stores, such as Nordiska Kompaniet.

Another iconic design, the Berså, a white porcelain cup adorned with a repetitive design of simple dark green leaves connected by black lines, is the ubiquitous retro coffee set. That set, as well as Lindberg's Röd Aster, which came later in the 1970s, are decorated with floral prints reflective of a decade famous for bright colors and flower power. These cups remain popular today because Lindberg's designs are "easy to feel comfortable with," says Strandberg. "I think it's also important that they keep year after year." That is, enduring designs are easy to fall in love with, both because they remain visually appealing in modern kitchens, but also because they transport us back to a time and place before computers and smartphones, where long coffee breaks carried on uninterrupted.

Vintage dishware is hip in its own right, and lends a youthful, modern kitchen a throwback flair. But deep nostalgia still lies with the delicate porcelain of Rörstrand sets. Founded in 1726, Rörstrand remains one of Europe's oldest porcelain factories. Today, at large department stores in Sweden, you can still find one of the company's quintessential designs: Mon Amie. Painted on a field of white, blue flowers transport the drinker to the middle of a Swedish meadow of summer wildflowers. But the design's uplifting style and popularity also lies in its history. "The pattern was something quite new in post-[World War II] Sweden…they yearned for something else, something fresher and happier," says Jenny Ljungblom of the Rörstrand Museum, which houses many of the classic cups and plates produced by Rörstrand.

"People often relive previous experiences through the things that they have around them, and porcelain is often an important part of that," says Strandberg. "Who doesn't remember the afternoon parties at grandma's house in the countryside when we were little? You remember what cups and plates she used to serve, don't you? Porcelain helps us to remember smells, tastes, and emotions from years ago."

Contemporary Swedish coffee cup designers still look to those old designs to draw inspiration and retool tradition. "Swedish design has a sense of simplicity and honesty. It feels clean, with no fuss, and no complicated patterns or shapes. We believe it also feels harmonic and calm, which can be a nice break compared to the complex world and society we live in today," says Rym Tounsi, founder of the contemporary design firm House of Rym, which produces a variety of coffee cups with modern, simple designs.

At the chic House of Rym boutique in Södermalm, the designs look familiar. They have hints of Lindberg, but are distinctly 2016. They are sleek, ergonomic, and less dainty—evocative of the historically clean Swedish designs inspired by nature, but with a modern twist. They have big, bold patterns but shapes you may see at a hip third wave coffee shop. And they serve as a festive foil to the austerity of the pure glass or wooden mugs lining the shelves of stores like Design Torget. House of Rym's designs are for more modern times, when coffee breaks with friends have become less ceremonious occasions.

Ljungblom views porcelain fika sets as an easy way to keep age-old rituals alive: "Meals are perhaps the only time of day when we sit down and relax for a while. It is nice to do so with china that you have inherited from someone close to you." Even for those who don't inherit a set, there's a pull towards the classic designs now being repurposed for modern production. And those who do inherit find themselves pulling out the porcelain more often than they would have initially expected. They may not have purchased the fragile dishware at a store, but once it's been passed down, it comes with added value that extends beyond pure aesthetics.

For most, a high-quality dinner service with beautiful plates, bowls, and cutlery isn't feasible every day. A beautiful coffee cup, however, is easy to incorporate, and a low-maintenance form of self-expression. "How you drink your coffee is very individual, as is your choice of cup," says Tounsi. "Drinking coffee is a habit and a routine people have every day and your everyday items are special to us. People choose their cups based on the mood they're in, based on the type of occasion it is—for example a Monday evening at home versus a Saturday dinner with friends."

Whether it's new or old, what a beautiful coffee cup says is, "I care about this drink." Coffee quickly becomes not just a special occasion, but also a memorable one. With a beautiful coffee cup, drinking coffee goes from mere routine to cherished ritual, one that we just might pass down from this generation to the next. Because, thinking back on the moments I have spent with my grandmother on her balcony drinking coffee together, I may not remember what the coffee tasted like, or the youthful yet understated elegance of her expressions, but I'll always remember the smooth, unblemished cups, and the weight of them in my hands. •

Lattes On Leave

WORDS Angela Almeida and John Surico
PHOTOGRAPHS Adam Goldberg and Daniela Velasco

Not far from the Hornstull stop, in the cafe-lined district of Södermalm, Mia Öhrn was enjoying her day off. Stationed in her kitchen studio, known as the Matlabbet ("The Food Lab"), she had just finished baking seven types of traditional Swedish cookies for a magazine photo shoot the next day. And now, just after noon, it's time for fika.

She fixed us a French press. "My career means very much to me. I didn't want to stop working," she said. "So this month, on Mondays, Tuesdays and Fridays, I'm here [at the studio]."

As a freelance food writer and pastry chef in Stockholm, Mia knows she cannot afford to take too much time off. Luckily, under Sweden's parental leave policy, the mother of two doesn't have to: "Today," she continued, "my husband is home with my sons."

Sweden's social welfare system makes it one of the most generous countries in the world—especially for those with newborns. New parents think in terms of the magic number 480: the total number of days they are afforded paid parental leave by the government, which is 80 percent of their salary for the first 390 days and a flat fee after that. And, for many parents like Mia and her husband, those allotted days can be divided up however they see fit until the child is eight years old.

That leaves a substantial amount of time for Swedes, both men and women, to be at home all day—but that doesn't necessarily mean their social circles have to be abandoned. Instead, a great number of parents can be found at their local oases, huddled over cups of coffee, maintaining a sacred tradition.

"Fika is central when you are on parental leave, because you're extremely tired, and you need tons of strong coffee," Öhrn, whose sleep schedule is still in flux, explained.

Whether you're in the historic district of Gamla Stan, or the more residential, upscale neighborhood of Östermalm, it's hard not to notice strollers, or prams, lining the sidewalks outside of nearly every cafe. "I think there are two or three cafes in all of Stockholm that don't have high chairs for babies," Öhrn joked. That's because, huddled inside, swapping stories of breast-feeding and late-night wake up calls, are the resilient clans of latte-mammas and latte-pappors, as they've been classified by Swedes and the rest of the world.

When asked how often she fikas, Emma Sundh—a latte-mamma by day, freelance journalist by night—exclaimed, "Every day!"

Emma and her husband, John, decided to split parental leave in half beginning the day their daughter Majken was born. At first, this meant Emma switched off with John on certain days. After the first few months, however, they divided their time in larger portions.

"Everybody says that the first few years—and even the first few months—are when so much happens for the baby, so we really wanted to be there every step of the way," John told us. What they didn't want was one person filling the other in on everything at the end of the day. "Not like one of us coming home, not having a clue about what the other person has been doing, or what taking care of the baby is like at all."

But this one-on/one-off daily division of labor is unorthodox for Swedish parents. According to several subjects we spoke with, the mother is typically the first to take time off—usually in the baby's early infancy—while the father takes over closer to when the baby is nearly a year old. "John has [weekly] meet-ups at cafes with dads that have just taken their leave," Emma said. "Because at nine, 10, or 11 months, most parents switch."

Although it's become incredibly commonplace to see fathers like John strolling their children down the streets of Stockholm, it wasn't always like that.

When Sweden became the first country to extend maternity leave to both parents, in 1974, it was taboo for fathers to take their afforded time off, so much so that they were nicknamed "velvet dads," a jab at their presumed femininity. By 1991, the problem persisted, and in order to bridge the gender gap, the Swedish state launched campaigns aimed at masculinizing

mode
kaffè
konst
mat

fatherhood, which included ads showing weightlifters benching babies.

Still, that wasn't enough for equal parenting to take shape. That's why, in 1995, the Swedish government went a step further, introducing "daddy leave," an incentive that meant families lost a month's worth of paid parental leave if fathers chose not to take time off. The mandate worked: soon after, eight in 10 men stayed home, even if only for a short time.

Since then, the larger societal conversation has focused not only on expanding that paternal role, but the importance of parental leave itself. In 2002, the Swedish government offered a bonus to parents: if they each took at least two months' leave, they would earn an extra two months at home. As of this year, fathers are now required to take a minimum of three months paid leave.

Over the course of nearly four decades, what started off as 180 days just for mothers has ballooned to 480 days, ideally split between both parents. At the core of these policy changes is Sweden's continued pursuit of gender equality—an issue that has placed the Scandinavian country at the forefront of disrupting conventional modern roles.

"In Sweden, it is not considered acceptable to dismiss something as 'women's work' or 'men's work,'" said James Savage, the managing editor of The Local, an English-speaking news network based in Stockholm.

In Sweden, everything from children's textbooks to shower gels are reviewed for gender stereotypes. There is also a growing call in the Swedish government to ban any advertisements that are deemed sexist, or exploiting female sexuality for the sake of selling a product. And in July of 2015, hen, a gender-neutral pronoun, was added to Swedish Facebook in an effort to be more inclusive.

"[Whether it's] due to parental leave, or whether parental leave is a symptom of these attitudes, it's hard to discern what the chicken is, and what the egg is," Savage said. This chicken-or-egg debate belies the deeper economic realities that parental leave seeks to address.

According to most mothers we spoke with, the policy protects their careers—meaning that, once they have a baby, they are not quarantined to the kitchen. In doing so, the Swedish state strives to ensure that women stay in the workforce. Add in the fact that state-subsidized daycare is available for children when they turn one, which makes it that much easier for mothers to return to work.

"It's important for women and our economic freedom," Emma Sundh explained. "It's important to share [parenting responsibilities], so you don't take a step back in your career or salary."

However, what may appear as parental paradise has its reality checks: Several subjects we spoke with said some employers discourage parents from taking months-long leave, even though this practice is illegal. In a more severe case, one subject said a friend had recently been fired for taking paternity leave. The reason? The business had just been acquired by an American company. (To note: America is one of the only developed countries in the world that does not mandate paid parental leave.)

There is also still a problem of unequal pay in Swedish society. Men earn more than their female counterparts, and so, taking time off can be an obstacle for many. Even now, when nine out of 10 Swedish fathers take paid parental leave, women still claim about 75 percent of those days off.

When it comes to fika, however, latte-mammas and latte-pappors find equal ground. That's why, young 20- and 30-something men and women are washing down kanelbullar with coffee in equal numbers at cafes all over Stockholm. Participating in an integral part of Swedish culture doesn't disappear during parenthood. And, even though there's still room to grow, if you drop by Fabrique Stenugnsbageri at 1 pm on a weekday, you'll have to weave through strollers and tables of new parents, male and female, chatting over coffee. And it becomes clear as day: The policies are working. •

Little Big Ear

WORDS Annalisa Rosso

"If our objects (and buildings) were people in a room, they wouldn't be the loudest people there; they would be the most interesting once you got to know them a little better—and you would never tire of their friendship," says Eero Koivisto, one of the founders of the design and architecture firm Claesson Koivisto Rune based in Stockholm. Whether the firm is designing an enormous building or a tiny object to hold sugar cubes, the overarching philosophy remains the same: "The work should be unobtrusive, but still carry a certain personality in its appearance. Our work should be able to coexist with other designs," he says.

But can the firm lauded worldwide as *the* Swedish minimalists, as the epitome of contemporary design, co-exist with an Italian designer tasked with creating coffee cups?

The firm's founders, Mårten Claesson, Eero Koivisto, and Ola Rune, met Luca Nichetto, an Italian industrial designer from Venice, a few years ago when he began working in Stockholm. They poke fun at each other, highlighting the cultural gulfs between the subdued Swedes and the emotive Italians. "We always make a little fun of the differences between the Swedes and Italians," says Nichetto. "Even with regard to how coffee is drunk."

They always talk about coffee.

Even the espresso cup is a topic for debate. Italian espresso cups come with saucers, but there's no such thing in Stockholm. So, when Koivisto asked Nichetto to design a piece for the 2016 collection of the firm's brand Smaller Object, Koivisto hinted that he wanted to see Nichetto design an espresso cup that would settle the debate once and for all. "We only put a cup into production—no saucer, the Swedish way," explains Nichetto. "Who knows? Maybe one day I'll add a saucer. For me, as an Italian, a cup is naked without it."

Why get an Italian to design a Swedish coffee cup? "What interested us was the mix of Italian and Scandinavian design, which is apparent in Luca's work," says Koivisto. Indeed, the cup marries, in the form of a small object, the typical simplicity of Swedish design with traditional Italian Industrial Design.

Nichetto drinks a lot of coffee: filter coffee in the studio, which here is a cultural norm, and coffee made at home with the Italian Moka pot in the morning. "Ever since I met my wife, who is Swedish, I've almost completely cut out milk and sugar, which is the norm here. Now I have a completely different perception of the flavor, one unaltered by sweetness."

Nichetto's first cup for Smaller Object made its debut in Stockholm in February 2016 at the Stockholm Supplies & Light Fair. He called it Little Big Ear, named for the peculiar handle on the espresso cup. The handle doesn't have a hole through which a coffee drinker could slide an index finger; the hole has been filled and the only way to hold the cup is by pinching it between the thumb and forefinger. It's elegant, sleek, and interactive—the design almost makes it impossible to hold for an extended period of time with one hand only. Both hands need to participate and feel the weight of the delicate yet sturdy porcelain body of the cup. Nichetto may be Venetian, but Little Big Ear is Scandinavian minimalism to a T.

The Swedish design movement began in the early 20th century, with the publication of its manifesto: *Vackrare vardagsvara (More Beautiful Everyday Things)* by Greger Paulsson, an art historian and secretary of the Swedish Society of Industrial Design. Today, that not-for-profit association is called Svensk Form (The Swedish Society of Crafts and Design) and is mandated by the Swedish government to promote Swedish design at home and abroad. The democratic design ideals of that manifesto made Stockholm one of the most relevant centers of production in the world—with IKEA as a shining example.

Smaller Object, founded in 2015 and operated by Claesson Koivisto Rune to sell long-term and well-designed everyday objects, operates within that context. "I wanted to do something simple," says Nichetto. "The products of this brand have a strong personality, and at the same time must be timeless." The big hurdle was making his design stand out from billions of other cups, while making sure the design had a long shelf life. Add to that his frustration with the lack of ergonomics in coffee drinking: "We often see people drinking coffee grasping the cup in a strange way, even holding it with the whole hand."

His handle, instead, resembles pinched fresh clay, approximately the size of your fingers. It rests comfortably in the human hand, just as Nichetto intended, "I wanted to design an object that would combine its strong aesthetic form with proportions able to influence and educate the gestures of the user."

This isn't the first time that the firm was tasked with designing with fika in mind. In 2013, Claesson Koivisto Rune took on the Ceremony Project for Mjölk design gallery, based in Toronto, which also works on the production of objects. "We wanted to add useful pieces to the ceremony of having coffee, a relevant social encounter with pieces that normally aren't very 'design-y,' and are rather functional." For instance, they produced a tray partially cast in metal to to help retain heat. Then there was a ceramic pitcher, which had a wooden lid that doubled as a small bowl for sugar cubes or cookies.

"Having coffee is a part of life, and many times it's a perfect micro-break for collecting your thoughts and taking ideas further. Early in the morning the extra energy is not bad either," Koivisto jokes. He remembers his first cup vividly. "I was standing at a coffee bar in San Babila square in Milan during my first visit to the salon there. I felt I had truly *arrived*." Nichetto jumps in: "I must have been five or six years old when my grandmother gave me my first taste." Then he pauses, and laughs. "Perhaps it's true that we always talk about coffee?".

Underground

PHOTO ESSAY Adam Goldberg

Mesmerized by the vibrant reds and greens of Stockholm's most captivating paintings, you'll forget that there's no natural light. You're close to 30 meters underground, in the city's Tunnelbana (T-bana) stations, dwarfed by murals covering the craggy rock walls of the metro tunnels. For most city-dwellers, the art just recedes into the background, part of the humdrum of their weekday commutes. But you know better: This may be the world's longest museum—close to 110 kilometers in length—so you (and your coffee) aren't just passing through.

Fikanomics

WORDS Angela Almeida and John Surico
PHOTOGRAPHS Adam Goldberg

On a balmy Tuesday afternoon in Stockholm, Hannes Sjöblad swooped into the cafeteria of Epicenter on his hoverboard. The office had just finished lunch, and employees were refueling with afternoon coffees. "What vodka is for the Russians," Hannes explained, " fika is for the Swedes."

Epicenter, or Stockholm's first "House of Innovation," is a 15,000-square-foot tech incubator in the heart of the city. It provides space to some of the most prominent developers in the world, including Twitter, Google, and Yahoo. It's also a glimpse into the future. Robots roll around with animated holograms of employees. Doors open in response to radio-frequency identification chips implanted into several employees' hands. Hannes, Epicenter's "chief disruption officer," showed his off with glee.

Many call Sweden the second Silicon Valley, because it is home to companies like Spotify, Minecraft, and Candy Crush. But Epicenter, with its communal space and workflow, gets at something deeper. "We wanted to create a new heart in Stockholm based on innovation," Ola Ahlvarsson, one of Epicenter's founders, told us, "That is, focusing on modern values that we think the office of the future needs in order to inspire people to keep going to work."

Across Sweden, tech companies and non-tech companies are refining what they believe to be an ideal office environment. Here, there is a tangible obsession with the idea of a work-life balance: How can we get people to work better—and be happier?

Coffee is at the core of this push for perfection.

"Swedish companies foster very positive relationships between employees and employers," Mike Hecker said. "The best way to show that is through things that seem obvious. How is the work environment? How are the desks? How are the chairs? The phones? But the clearest way to show your appreciation is through coffee."

This is what Hecker does for a living: convince companies that fika, or the art of the coffee break, is beneficial—not only for the employees, but for employers, too. Hecker was one of the first marketing managers of Nespresso, and he helped promote the luxury coffee machine that has since taken Europe by storm. Now, he's CEO of Premium Coffee Holdings, or Hemi SA, which is in charge of distributing Nespresso to offices throughout the Nordic region.

And that shouldn't be a challenge, considering Scandinavian countries today consume the most coffee in the world.

"People all over the world quench their thirst with water. How do Swedes quench their thirst instead?" he asked us. "Coffee."

In the Swedish workplace, the centuries-old tradition of fika is a cultural mandate. Employers are legally required to provide five minutes of break time for every hour; so, naturally, employees combine those five-minute breaks, taking a 15-minute break in the morning, and another in the afternoon, to stop whatever it is they're doing to sit down, talk, and drink coffee together.

This isn't just part of startup culture either: Offices across all industries are equipped with a room for fika, sometimes separate from the cafeteria. Many even come equipped with an in-house barista, and offer everything from drip coffee to cortados.

As a more modern form of watercooler culture, fika in the workplace is seen as a way to strengthen employee relationships, and to take a break in their busy workdays to recharge. Maximizing productivity is the idea here— or just finding that formula of how to make the office function better. "You actually have studies by big consulting companies, like Bain [Capital]," Hecker added, "that show a clear correlation between the quality of a coffee break and companies' productivity."

For Johanna Kindvall, a Swedish-born illustrator, fika wasn't necessarily optional. "I had bosses who would get really upset if I didn't show up for fika," she told us.

When Kindvall worked in Gothenburg and Lund, the coffee break was an integral part of the day, both for planning and coordination. "It's also the time you talk about things in the office, like details for an upcoming party, or preparations for a conference," she continued. "It's a social thing, but it's also an office gathering."

So, when Kindvall moved to New York, where she now lives, not having that meeting time was confounding. At one job, she said, a fellow employee asked aloud if anyone wanted coffee. "I answered like a Swede," she told us, laughing. "I was like, 'Oh yeah, great, coffee!'" She later found out that it was an empty gesture, not an invitation. "I thought, 'When is the coffee? You haven't told me when the coffee is. Have they done it without me?'"

She looked around for it. "They just made a pot in the back, and took it back to their offices," she continued. "When I got there, the coffee was already finished."

What Kindvall describes is a classic cultural clash between the American and Swedish workplaces,

or, in particular, the value placed on workers versus their time at work. It also highlights the difference in philosophies of efficiency, bearing the ultimate question: Does working longer hours, without taking breaks, equate to greater output? Or does an emphasis on fika, vis-à-vis human interaction, improve productivity?

According to 2014 data, apparently it's the former: In terms of productivity per employee, Sweden falls behind the U.S. Out of 38 countries, Sweden is ranked 11th, while the U.S. comes in fourth. But on the other side of the scale, it's a different story: In the latest World Happiness Report, Sweden is 10th in the world. The U.S.? 13th.

In recent years, some Swedish industries have gone even further to address this question of targeted efficiency by experimenting with a six-hour workday, in order to see if this is the ideal amount of time in which to capture workers' full potential. And, in America, there is a visible push to incorporate new ideas into old models: Tech companies and startups are starting to resemble places like Epicenter in their reimagining of what a modern office should look like, with a litany of frothy coffee options from which to choose.

This is especially true for American companies that wish to employ in Stockholm.

"One of our biggest successes is with American companies [in Sweden] because they understand fika is the easiest, lowest-cost employee motivator," Hecker told us. "I find American companies in the Nordic countries adapt very fast."

Needless to say, the two countries—all countries, for that matter—can learn from each other, to perfect that work-life balance as our modern-day concepts of productivity continue to change. But if there's one thing we can take from the Swedes, it is this: a little coffee every now and then never hurt anyone. •

Rocking the Oat

WORDS Lucas Oswald
PHOTOGRAPHS Adam Goldberg and Daniela Velasco

Last August, 4,000 people gathered in Stockholm to celebrate specialty coffee at the annual Kaffefestivalen, which took place over the course of three days in a 150-year-old theater. Attendees could be found roasting green coffee beans in pans over open fire, smearing coffee onto canvases at the "Paint With Coffee" station, or getting their fortunes told via clairvoyant inspection of coffee grounds. An art installation featuring an espresso machine rigged with microphones amplified its gurgles and hisses, so that even the sound of coffee could be fully appreciated. Yet amid the absurdities, one thing was conspicuously missing: milk. In all of the places you would expect to find it, you found oat milk instead.

Oat milk is the most popular non-dairy alternative in Sweden. Made from soaking steel cut oats or whole groats in water, blending the mixture, then straining it, oat milk is slightly thicker than soy milk with a creamy texture and semi-sweet flavor. It's reminiscent of the toasty, congealed layer that floats atop morning porridge—an association many Swedes are quick to make, especially because oat milk is best enjoyed steamed.

Lately, it has given soy milk the boot.

Specialty coffee is built on the scrupulous consideration of the entire coffee production process, from the terroir to the temperature of a pour over. Combine this with Sweden's deeply ingrained environmentalism, and it is no wonder that soy milk came under scrutiny.
Cafes that valued coffee producers who proved to be good stewards of their land began to question the origins of soy milk, mostly mass produced by companies that provided little to no transparency in their production processes. Though soy milk didn't come with the cost concerns of almond milk, for example, mass soybean cultivation practices are murky at best—and numerous studies have questioned the consequences of frequent consumption.

"How is the soy being made? On what terms is the soy being provided to us?" asked Joel Wredlert, owner and manager of Kafé Esaias and Kafé Orion. "You start to question that the same way that you question 'How is this coffee bean here in Stockholm?'" Shop owners weren't completely comfortable with the answers—or lack thereof.

Now, at cafes all over Stockholm, baristas don't even flinch when customers request a latte made with oat milk instead of cow's milk. In fact, at Johan & Nyström, customers will find a special menu dedicated to cleverly named oat drinks, such as the Cap*oat*chino, the C*oat*ado, and the Macchi*oato*, just in case customers needed it spelled out.

A company called Oatly is at least partially responsible for the alternative milk's popularity. Built on superb branding, Oatly postures itself as both friendly and revolutionary. The company comes off as refreshingly anti-corporate, evoking the messaging of a mom-and-pop shop concerned with combatting the shady practices of the big, bad corporate milk industry. Promoting oat milk's health benefits, low price, and dedication to environmental responsibility, Oatly quickly established itself as the Swedish choice of milk alternatives, not just because it is produced and processed in Sweden, but because it reflects the Swedish conscience and consideration of the broader implications of their consumer choices.

According to Wredlert, Oatly's popularity "is mostly about identity." That is, "being able to question every single bit of the drink and make it your own" made it particularly appealing to Swedish culture.

But quality always comes first. For milk substitutes, that means flavor, texture, and the ability to steam and froth for espresso drinks. Good milk must foam when steamed and, unlike almond milk, which runs the risk of taking on a burnt flavor when heated, oat milk stands up to the heat and even supports intricate latte art. It also helps that oat milk tastes good—sweet, toasty, a little grassy. Wredlert mentions that it "isn't overly sweet or excessively heavy."

"We had no reason not to work with it," says Wredlert. "It was creamy. It kicked ass ethically and politically compared with soy. It was the same price. Suddenly oat milk just took over."

Wredlert ascribes that speedy success to increased visibility during a contentious debate Oatly incited in the international press. Discussions around the alternative milk veered "a little bit political," as Oatly launched a series of advertisements taking aim at the dairy industry. Playing the underdog, Oatly campaigned with taglines that read: "No milk, no soy, no badness"; "It's like milk, but made for humans"; and "Wow, no cow!" Soon after those advertisements, the Swedish Dairy Association, Svensk Mjölk, filed a lawsuit against Oatly, claiming that the advertisements falsely discredited milk as unhealthy. Oatly's star continued to rise.

By the time Svensk Mjölk formally won the lawsuit in October, 2014, Oatly had already won over public opinion. As those proceedings dragged on in court, Oatly cleverly publicized all the details of the lawsuit online, framing the milk industry as a greedy corporate bully. Loyal Oatly consumers retaliated with the slogan "Team Oatly." It became fashionable to support the brand, and you can still spot the occasional "Post-Milk Generation" tee on stylish young people in Stockholm. By the time the lawsuit was over, Oatly's Swedish sales had increased 43 percent in just one year. Referring to the lawsuit, Oatly's CEO boldly told Bloomberg, "Maybe I should have tried it before."

Despite the drama, oat milk owes its popularity to Swedish tradition. "Oat is closer to our hearts," said Wredlert, comparing it to soy. "Oats are in the porridge you eat in the morning, a classic breakfast in Sweden. Oats are what we use to make our chocolate balls [the classic Swedish dessert, chokladbollar]. Oats are in our muesli."

Unlike milk made from soy, rice, or almond, oat milk is recognizable—like a warm, comforting hug from an old friend on a cold winter's day. Whether Swedes buy oat milk for environmental reasons, for kids' school lunches, or for the satisfaction of taking down the dairy industry, the flavor remains familiar. "Oat," continued Wredlert, "is just so easy to accept." •

THE ORIGINAL

OAT-LY!

iKAFFE

HAVREDRYCK
ATT SKUMMA

100% cool
for vegans.

1L

it's Swe-dish!

Fair
Game

WORDS Micha Van Dinther
PHOTOGRAPHS Mikael Axelsson

In almost any coffee shop, in almost any part of the world, the coffee is sourced, roasted, ground, and brewed by men. But in Stockholm, chances are that women have been involved with at least part of the process. Beginning in preschool, Swedish children are inculcated with the idea that men and women are equals. The earliest inklings of that ethos date as far back as the 1200s, when King Birger Jarl passed a law forbidding violence against women, marking a new era in the perception of womanhood. By 1974, Sweden became the first country in the world to replace maternity leave with gender-neutral parental leave. And in 1980 the constitutional monarchy retooled the Act of Succession to ensure the current king, Carl XVI Gustaf, would be succeeded by his eldest child, the Crown Princess Victoria, and not his eldest son, as would have been the case in the past.

These days, the focus on progressive gender equality in Sweden—though not fully realized—has created a culture that encourages women to take jobs in traditionally male-dominated spaces. It has allowed Joanna Alm, Sara Hjälmås, and Ida Carlsson to make names for themselves in the hyper-macho world of specialty coffee, where the number of milligrams of caffeine a barista can withstand is sometimes viewed as a proxy for intensity and skill. It doesn't even faze Alm, Hjälmås, and Carlsson: They're at the top of their games.

Joanna Alm, CEO and head roaster of Drop Coffee

"My main driving force is my belief that I can always make a better cup of coffee. That's it, plain and simple."

That's Joanna Alm, CEO and head roaster of renowned roaster and cafe Drop Coffee, and she's joining me over a quick cup of Chorongi, a coffee originating from the Nyeri region of central Kenya. Seated at a cupping table at her sparsely decorated roaster in the Västberga industrial area of Stockholm, she allows herself a few minutes to breathe between a lecture she gave earlier today and an afternoon full of client meetings. Steering Stockholm's most esteemed roaster means that Alm's schedule is hectic to say the least. But the idea of brewing a better cup, and a desire to push progress in the industry—in Sweden, yes, but also in the communities of bean farmers abroad—sustain her.

She started her career in Oslo, Norway. To get a better lay of the land, she did what any of us would do. She typed a simple query into Google: "Best coffee in Oslo." The result pointed her to Tim Wendelboe, the Norwegian roaster who was months away from opening his now-legendary coffee bar. It was 2007 when she decided to track him down.

"When we finally met, he gave me a Kenyan coffee that just blew my mind," says Alm. "I just couldn't figure out how coffee could taste so strongly of black currant."

The eye-opener triggered several questions: What differentiates beans grown in different regions? If one coffee could taste of black currant, what were the other possibilities? How were the growers treated? How could a barista extract maximum and optimal flavor from a bean?

She set up an origin trip; it was time to trace the intriguing bean back to its roots, first in Costa Rica then in Panama. If she hoped to be the last link in the chain before the final product reached customers, then she wanted to know everything about the process—and make sure that the farmers she worked with were being treated fairly. To this day, those grower trips are one of her favorite parts of the job.

After-hours, Alm competes. She won the Swedish Coffee Roasting Championship in 2014 and 2016, and took second place in the World Coffee Roasting Championship in 2015. "For me, part of it is about exposing myself and taking risks, but I mostly want to push for progress," says Alm, who is usually the only female contestant. Even though Stockholm's coffee scene is more female-friendly than what Alm has witnessed elsewhere in the world, she wants more women to join the industry.

"When I started out a little over 10 years ago, I had to defend my line of work. People referred to me as a cafe worker. Now that being a barista is considered a hip occupation, only men do it. But there are so many talented women in the coffee industry who need more exposure."
According to Alm, the industry would make better coffee if more women's voices were heard. While Swedish men engage in destructive, competitive showdowns, there's an ongoing dialogue between female roasters in the city. She describes it as "open and courteous," and says that Stockholm's female roasters share a willingness to exchange information and recipes. She thinks it may be why Sweden's rapidly growing coffee scene has been strong from the start.

Sara Hjälmås, SCEA-certified judge, podcast host of Filterkaffe, and coffee purveyor at Johan & Nyström

Swedes recognize Sara Hjälmås. She was only 19 when she sang her heart out in front of the jury members of the talent show Swedish Idol on national television. Originally a musician from Gothenburg, Sweden's second largest city, Hjälmås first got into the coffee business to pay the bills.

"I got hooked at my first coffee job working at one of the larger coffee chains. I loved how I got to work with my hands and all of my senses," remembers Hjälmås, seated in a large armchair at one of the Johan & Nyström outposts in town. "When I'm at the coffee machine, I feel as though I'm on stage."

Her first barista gig was at Johan & Nyström in Stockholm, and to this day, she loves the coffee retailer that for its willingness to rethink the coffee business. Not long after starting there, she began competing, hoping that competitions would give her the adrenaline rush she used to get while performing. "I started out as a spectator, trying to decide if I should get into the game," she says. "But I learned I don't have the nerves for it, so I found another way to contribute with my knowledge by judging the national coffee championship two years in a row." And she liked that: talking about coffee, where the industry is going, what quality in coffee should mean.

She also enjoyed attending competitions because she kept running into writer Ulrika Ingemarsdotter. The two hit it off immediately. Despite both being women, Hjälmås describes her relationship with Ingemarsdotter as a "bromance." "We would often discuss what it was like being women in coffee. Our talks didn't stem from a feeling of being in the minority—it was more about finding our place, and brainstorming ways to make a contribution," explains Hjälmås.

But as satisfying as it was to talk about the issues, the two wanted to share their thoughts with a wider audience. By 2015, the duo launched a podcast, Filterkaffe, dedicated to coffee. They've earned a loyal following, and have become known for their thoughtful discussions on everything from fair-trade and ecological certifications to examining creativity in the industry.

"If I were to generalize, getting the respect one deserves takes longer as a woman—especially if, like me, you are blonde and like to wear lipstick," notes Hjälmås. "When I meet other judges, especially when I'm abroad, they make note of the fact that I'm a woman who dares to make myself heard." Bucking stereotypes is an everyday battle for Hjälmås. And, though it isn't getting any easier, she's getting a lot better at dismissing the haters. "I've learned not to listen too much to what others say—I just do whatever I need and want to do for myself."

Ida Carlsson, barista at AB Kafé

"I remember it like it was yesterday: It was an AeroPress Panama Geisha from Hacienda la Esmeralda." That was the cup that changed everything for Ida Carlsson, who, at the time, didn't even drink coffee.

Born and raised in the northern city of Kiruna, she started working at a tiny cafe in the region of Dalarna right after secondary school, in a time when specialty coffee hadn't reached Sweden yet. "Sure, I would prepare the coffee and knew how it should taste. I just never really cared for it myself."

But, years later, after that Panama Geisha, she was was a coffee believer. She stopped by Johan & Nyström for a coffee, to see if the renowned shop would be able replicate that initial eye-opening experience, and realized she might want to work there. A few months later, she was hired. Now, Carlsson is at AB Kafé in Midsommarkransen, an outer borough of Stockholm. "Good coffee, good fika, and a welcoming vibe—that's what it's all about. Each neighborhood in Stockholm has it's own local way of drinking coffee, and in Telefonplan, where AB Kafé is located, people like to grab a sit-down fika." It's way different from her previous gig at Mean Coffee, a now-defunct coffee shop that sourced its beans from Northern

European roasters and found its niche catering to hurried commuters at Stockholm Central Station in need of to-go cups.

A self-proclaimed creative, Carlsson now concerns herself with creating the complete experience: from the design and location to the food and service. The experience at AB Kafé is slow and deliberate, just the way she intends it to be. Because of this attention to detail—and her charisma—her customers are fiercely loyal to Carlsson, following her from shop to shop. She's whip-smart and outspoken; you can't help but listen, really listen, to what she says. She's commanding.

"My success in a male-dominated industry all comes down to my personality," she says, "I'm a daredevil. My mother is a strong woman and I've gotten the courage to stand up for myself from my upbringing."

Carlsson appreciates that Stockholm-based women in the coffee business really push each other. She believes that injecting a female point of view into the machismo of coffee shops will help them grow and mature. And, by creating a space where women feel welcomed and prized for their skills as baristas, the coffee might even taste better too. "You know," Carlsson elbows, "a beard and lots of tattoos aren't essential to being a good barista."•

Stories from a Changing Sweden

WORDS Andrew Cole
PHOTOGRAPHS Adam Goldberg and Daniela Velasco

Fika 1: Ola's House, Stocksund.

The light-filled living room was a welcomed change from the airplane. Stockholm's fantastic infrastructure had practically carried us, door-to-door, from the terminal to an elaborate fika spread: saffron Christmas cookies, coffee, and tea. Arabian-influenced music floated through the house.

I came to Sweden to see how the country was managing the wave of refugees currently bottlenecking at its borders and processing centers. My trip started with a history lesson from our host, Ola Ahlvarsson. First lesson: Fika is a distinctly Swedish experience. It's not just coffee and pastries, but also conversation.

If Sweden's forward-thinking global ambitions could be distilled into one person, it would probably be Ola: In addition to his own business, Result, which helps companies break into new countries, he runs Stockholm's "House of Innovation," Epicenter, where he is frequently seen patrolling the halls on the screen of a roving robot. He is also one of the creators of Star Stable, an online game with over six million users (98 percent of them are young girls) who explore a virtual world with pony avatars. He is an exhaustingly fun person to be around, and an encyclopedic source of information on Sweden.

Inside his house, an airy, converted kindergarten in the tony Stockholm suburb of Stocksund, Ola explained that, since the early 19th century, the country has, in part, defined itself by its pacifism. More recently, this approach has manifested itself as a come-one-and-all breed of humanitarianism. In the 20th century, Sweden welcomed Bosnians, Kurds, Iranians, and Vietnamese refugees. Today, the roster at any Swedish company would include employees named from Akerman to Zetterborg, and Abadžić to Zabaneh as well.

Sipping his tea (milk, no sugar), Ola explained, "Sweden's attitude is: You help a drowning person because they are drowning, not because of their religion or race."

But Sweden has received an unprecedented wave of refugees in the last two years—more per resident capita than any country in Europe.

They have come from Syria, Iraq, Afghanistan, and elsewhere: places at war, where security is a privilege, not a given. "The difference now is that Sweden has never tried to save so many at once."

Integrating so many immigrants is not without its difficulties. Take, for example, male-female relations in the country. Sweden is ranked fourth in the world for gender equality (preceded only by its Scandinavian neighbors), according to the Global Gender Gap Report by the World Economic Forum. (At one coffee shop, out of habit, I made the mistake of holding the door open for a group of women queuing behind me. The bemused look they gave me was enough to know that antiquated ideals of chivalry had been happily buried in Sweden.)

Yet for many of Sweden's newest residents, talking to a woman at all is so strange that the difference between a compliment and a sexual advance is unrecognizable. One Swede we spoke to told us about an Uzbek friend of his who was invited to exercise with a female friend. The concept of doing something so intimate was, to him, a clear invitation for an advance. For her, nothing could be more mundane.

The awkward transition to life in Sweden has led to a growing sense of disenfranchisement amongst many first- and second-generation immigrants about their place in contemporary Swedish society. The implicit attitude toward immigrants, according to Ahlvarsson, has become something akin to: "You're welcome to come to my house for dinner, but you have to eat in the basement."

I wanted to see the view from the basement.

Fika 2: Nejo's Cafe, Rinkeby.

Rinkeby, seven miles from the city center, is a site of self-segregation for recent immigrants. It was erected in the 1980s as part of the Miljonprogrammet, a scheme to solve the housing shortage in post-war Sweden with cheap, standardized apartment buildings on the outskirts of major cities. Much like social housing in the United States, or Le Corbusier's architectural experiments on the outskirts of Paris, the Miljonprogrammet was largely a failure. Swedes didn't like living in the squat, featureless buildings that expressed little beyond rigid economic efficiency. Those who could, quickly opted to live elsewhere. Since the 1980s, the buildings have been reoccupied by recent arrivals to Sweden, and today in Rinkeby, 89.1 percent of the population is a first-generation or second-generation immigrant.

When we walked into Nejo's Cafe, it was like we had walked into a 19th century Western saloon: Heads turned and all went quiet as we opened the door. Everyone was Somali or Ethiopian, and male. We were the subjects of brief glances of inspection and curiosity. There was not a word of Swedish spoken.

What we heard instead was Rinkeby Swedish, a dialect that mixes Swedish with hip-hop terminology and Arabic exclamations—a product of the ethnic amalgam in the neighborhood. By the same token, what we saw at Nejo's could be called Rinkeby fika. Despite the fact that everyone in Nejo's Cafe was born outside of Sweden, and were speaking to people from their own country, they were doing what all Swedes do over coffee and pastries: complaining about their bosses, worrying about paying the bills, and laughing over jokes.

Like most cafes in Sweden, Nejo's had a pot of coffee sitting on the counter for free refills. Whenever the pot was refreshed, a line would form to fill up, illustrating two Swedish traditions: Swedes' claim to be the highest per capita consumers of coffee in the world, and their affinity for queuing ("Queueing is our national sport," quipped one Swede we met).

Judging by the furtive glances we were getting in line, the only strategy that would get us anywhere would be to step outside with the smokers, who seemed chattier. I queued, filled my cup, and proceeded outside.

"Are you French?" It's a good thing I'm not; Faysal was from Algeria, and had some unkind words for French involvement in his place of birth. "What are you doing in Rinkeby?" he then asked, somewhat befuddled by our presence there. Ours were the only European faces we had seen in the neighborhood.

"We're here to learn about Sweden." I said,

telling half of the truth. Before arriving in Stockholm, I had introduced myself online as a journalist to recent immigrants to Sweden. I was trying to make contacts, but I did not receive a single reply. I shouldn't have been surprised. As a refugee, it's better to lay low.

Faysal came to Sweden as a teenager. Like many recent immigrants from Syria, Afghanistan, and Iraq, he fled poverty and civil war. He had arrived alone in the late 1990s, and fit the profile of the lonely refugee against whom Swedes discriminated. Years later, that is no longer a concern for him. "My wife and I have assimilated, and my children are Swedish. I'm grateful to this country for what it's given me."

Teenage refugees, then and now, seem to embody many of the anxieties that Swedes hold about the refugee crisis—that the influx of immigrants, however deserving they are, threaten the marvelously functioning society that took generations for Sweden to build. Djurgården, a park in central Stockholm, is now avoided after dark due to supposed crime associated with young refugees. One Swede to whom we were introduced had been robbed more than once there. I asked Faysal, "Do you think that the teenagers coming here will be able to integrate like you have?"

"I think they will. And I think Sweden should help people from Syria. But the people coming from Afghanistan should stay at home. They're economic refugees. The war there is over. Sweden shouldn't let those people come." Fleeing poverty? No good, stay at home. Fleeing war? You're welcome to stay. Even refugees had a nuanced view of the refugee crisis.

Fikas 3 and 4: Bygdegård, Rinkeby.

Faysal was at Nejo's for a quick coffee before work. He took his drink black. As a black coffee drinker, I felt quite at home in Sweden. My friends and I said goodbye to Faysal, and we left to take a walk around Rinkeby.

It was a February day, the sky was a flat white, giving the bare trees and boxy buildings the look of having been pasted onto a piece of paper. We passed a number of women in chadors and men in skull caps with long shirttails that peeked out from under their parkas. Walking past a community center, we saw a sign in the window written in all-caps: "REFUGEES WELCOME."

The fika had been organized by Virginia, who had moved to Sweden 39 years ago from Pinochet's Chile. Children chased each other beneath murals of Native Swedes, Africans, Asians, and Middle Easterners holding hands. The church group included people from Chile, Ecuador, Egypt, Syria, and Leilah, who was from Iraq.

Leilah moved to Stockholm from Baghdad four months ago. Rather than taking the now-infamous route over land and water that has been in the news, Leilah had flown directly. She had converted to Christianity while still in Iraq, and life with her family in Baghdad became untenable as a result. A mission had sponsored her trip to Sweden, and she was staying with an Egyptian family in Rinkeby.

As she laid out cookies for the fika-goers, I could tell by the look in Leilah's eyes that she was still in shock that her life had changed so abruptly. But in this milieu, she fit right in. It was over fika that those in attendance, from all over the world, came together, implicitly espousing a deep gratitude to Sweden for welcoming them in their time of need.

Fika, for them, opened a forum: No matter where they came from, participating in Swedish culture helped them focus on their collective future as Swedes. It was a Swedish ritual they could understand and partake in; it was a common language everyone could master.

We had stumbled into the wrong fika. While refugees like Leilah were certainly welcomed by the Christian group, we had to walk to a library upstairs to join the fika advertised on the poster we had seen outside. Fika really does happen that often in Sweden.

In between the stacks, more women in chadors, men in skullcaps, and listless-looking teenagers read books and futzed around on desktop computers. On the walls, posters for classes looked promising. I asked Ingrid at the front desk about them. There had been an activity group for Afghan teenagers scheduled, but the only attendees were little girls accompanied by their parents. "Right now I'm working behind the desk," Ingrid said, "but I'm hosting a fika for people learning Swedish in four minutes," she said. She was punctual.

Before going to Sweden, I had hoped to meet some recent immigrants and host a fika myself. I was met with silence by everyone I asked. Until, by an amazing stroke of luck, I walked into that community center in Rinkeby. In four minutes, the Swedish government was about to do my job for me.

Nowhere in Stockholm did we find a better representation of fika as a vehicle for entry into Swedish society than in that library in Rinkeby. There, people who recently arrived from Turkey, Uzbekistan, Kenya, and Morocco, were being introduced to Swedish society over drip coffee (served out of brilliantly designed disposable mugs, no less), pastries, and children's books.

In the class, students' levels of comprehension varied.

I asked to take a photo. Right away, Viktor, from Uzbekistan, joked that he should have put makeup on. I looked at Fatima, an older woman in a hijab, to whom it suddenly dawned what this American stranger wanted to do. She grabbed her children's book and hid behind it, shooting a pleading glance at Ingrid. I put the camera away.

The book, from what I gathered, was about racism, homelessness, drugs, and alcohol. At one point, laughter broke out in the group. An important and poignant opportunity for a vocabulary lesson arose; there had been confusion over the words *alska* and *ilska*—"love" and "angry," respectively.

After the class, Hassane, the student from Morocco, helped me understand how, for immigrants to Sweden, the confusion between the two ideas goes beyond linguistics. His Swedish was so good (and mine is, admittedly, so bad) that, in the class, I thought he was one of the teachers. Swedish is just one of five languages he speaks, the others being French, Dutch, English, and the Arabic of his native Morocco.

I had found one of the "economic refugees" about whom Faysal had so much to say. Hassane was from Berkane, in northern Morocco. He had an undergraduate degree in economics from a Moroccan university. When he isn't working in a catering kitchen, he's taking night courses at a Swedish high school and language courses in Rinkeby, an hour from his home in Västerhaninge, a southern suburb of Stockholm. In our conversation, he oscillated between admiration and frustration for his adopted country.

"We are outsiders in the EU," he told me. "Everybody is afraid refugees will take their place—but I'm not like most refugees. I'm an exception." For Hassane, that distinction came with benefits and drawbacks. He had permission from the Swedish government to work and study, but was provided little in the way of help beyond that. It's a system that he repeatedly referred to as "stupid," and he had a point—a quintilingual economics student being forced to work as a gofer in a kitchen makes little economic sense. According to Hassane, Swedes seem to think "[refugees] will take things only to go back home. It isn't true. If Swedes want successful integration, something must change." But he had made a rational decision in immigrating, and admired much about his new home. Sweden "gives incredible opportunity to its citizens—here, I have the possibility to develop as an individual." Hassane approached immigration to Sweden as an economist would. "People need to understand that immigration is a gift. The economy will improve with these people. They will consume, more ideas will develop." Shaking his head, he told me, "Above

all, immigration creates wealth—not only economic, but cultural, human wealth."

There are signs of a thaw in Swedish society in this respect. During our history lesson, Ola told me that one cause of disenfranchisement is the lack of "role models" for many immigrant groups. "In London, there are several Somalis that have gone on to start successful businesses. In Stockholm, that just hasn't happened," and cloistered communities like Rinkeby can become hotbeds of frustration and resentment. He and his team at Epicenter are in the idea phase of an "immigrant university" designed to foster entrepreneurship amongst recent immigrants to Sweden. "The idea is to provide advice and funding to immigrant entrepreneurs, to create the kind of role models that could help entire neighborhoods" or immigrant groups. Saeid Esmailizadeh, who I met a few days later, was an example of how much Sweden could benefit from such a program.

Fika 5: Serendipity Innovations, Stureplan, Östermalm.

I had been told, when I met Saeid at dinner with our hosts in central Stockholm, that he was a "poster boy for successful Swedish immigration." We made plans to meet at his office two days later.

The next day, walking around Östermalm, I realized I wouldn't have trouble finding it. The name of his company, Serendipity Innovations, stretched in gigantic, green and white sans-serif lettering across the face of a building overlooking the mushroom at Stureplan, a concrete pavilion and common social gathering place in central Stockholm.

Entering the offices of Serendipity Innovations, a business incubator and investment firm focusing on breakthrough sciences, the term "poster boy" gained new meaning. The lobby was plastered in articles from the Swedish press featuring Saeid and his company.

I was greeted by Amin Omrani, CEO of Serendipity Innovations. He and Saeid both moved to Sweden from Iran as children following the Iranian Revolution. As I toured the office, Amin told me about the company. "We start businesses around breakthroughs in materials science," he explained to me as we toured the facilities. "We started out renting some rooms at the front of the building, and eventually occupied the full floor," he explained. "Then we expanded into the building next door," he told me, as we walked through a short glass bridge.

Saied joined us, tossing me a piece of ceramic that's used in the disk brakes of sports cars ("Is it in the Ferrari or the Lamborghini?" he asked

a nearby engineer). He also showed me a piece of foam that expands to 50 times its size when exposed to heat, making it extremely effective in extinguishing fires. While at Stockholm University, Saeid discovered the world's hardest glass, and began his career in business after patenting the process.

Over fikabröd and coffee in a conference room a few minutes later, I asked Saeid if, given the meteoric success of Serendipity Innovations, the wallpaper in the lobby described him as a successful Swede or as a successful immigrant. "As a successful immigrant," he quickly responded.

Amin and Saeid, who both grew up near Rinkeby where I had met Faysal, Leilah, and Hassane, were grateful for their dual identities. Their refugee background and their Swedish upbringing have synthesized: "I'm confident that trauma is the reason why we have built Serendipity," Saeid told me. "Whenever something is scary now, I reflect on it and think, 'How bad could this new thing really be?'"

At the same time, they expressed admiration for the way Swedish society has enabled them to succeed. "Sweden is successful because it is tolerant, open, adaptable, and has amazing infrastructure," Amin said. It was the "best place for an immigrant kid, because I could worry less and focus on creating value."

By their own admission, Saeid and Amin's path to success was made easier by the fact that they emigrated to Sweden at young ages. Their parents had a harder time adjusting to their adopted home. Saeid's father, a telecommunications CEO in Iran, has found it "tough to get a foothold to this day." Amin's father owns a grocery store. "Sweden is tolerant but closed," because immigrants "don't know the schnapps song"—again the concept of being invited to someone's home, but having to eat in the basement, arose. "Compare my parents to me and my sister," who is a neuroscientist and healthcare entrepreneur. "It was very tough for them," Saeid told me. "But it has been amazing for our generation." Despite Sweden's tolerance, however, one "wouldn't see a Swedish CEO listed on the stock exchange with an accent."

There is poignancy to the fact that my conversations about immigration in Sweden, made especially relevant by the recent wave of refugees from the Middle East, all took place over fika. A simple cup of coffee and an accompanying pastry signified an easy bridge between cultures that may not yet have seamlessly meshed.

As I watched the students in the fika in Rinkeby practice the foreign vowels of their adopted language, I was struck by the social rigidity reflected in the Miljonprogrammet architecture

outside, as well as the ingenuity of Swedes for having built disruption—fika—into the day. No other culture could simultaneously maintain its stability while welcoming rationed amounts of spontaneity.

Swedish culture has had a well-managed transition into modernity and globalization. It also has an outsized influence on the globe given its small geographic size and population. (Think: IKEA, Volvo, and Spotify.) And, despite the near-perfect English spoken by nearly everyone, Swedes still retain a real affinity for their own culture, "schnapps songs" and fika included. But the Swedish sense of duty towards those in need elsewhere in the world has never been seriously challenged, until now, when it is expected to welcome millions of people with open arms, perhaps at the expense of insular traditions.

The optimist in me hopes that Saeid and Amin represent the second generation of Swedish immigrants; that Hassane and Leilah represent the first; and that Faysal's children can grow up able to take the best of their immigrant backgrounds and Swedish upbringing to form a successful, peaceful package, perhaps with the help of forward-thinking Swedes like Ola, who understand the value these groups represent.

The years ahead will test the likelihood of that outcome. The number of new arrivals in Sweden are going to affect Swedish society as much as Swedish society will affect them. "Sweden has adapted, and people will adapt to Sweden," Saeid told me in his office. "But it will take time." •

DETTA HUS
BYGDES ANNO 1888

Fika Through The Ages

WORDS Angela Almeida and John Surico
PHOTOGRAPHS Adam Goldberg and Daniela Velasco

When we entered Sturekatten, an 18th-century konditori in Stockholm's Östermalm district, a narrow, winding staircase led up to the second floor. There, a dimly lit case of pastries and formally dressed servers awaited us. The ceilings were low in the cramped attic where we were seated, and candlelit chandeliers dangled above Victorian sofas. Visitors chatted quietly over creamy semlas and coffee, hiding away as if on an exclusive floor of a genteel, life-size dollhouse.

Looking around, Gustaf Eklöw, 17, remarked to us, "I'd only come to a place like this with my mom."

We met Eklöw a few weeks earlier over Skype after hearing about his school project. His teacher told the class to make a documentary about something inherently Swedish. He and his classmates chose fika. "We were gonna investigate fika," he told us, "with older and younger people—what fika is to them, how often they fika, and why it's so important for Swedes to fika."

What they found is that a konditori like Sturekatten was Old World: a traditional coffee shop that is more likely to attract older Swedes than hip young people. For teenagers, it is too formal, reserved, and expensive—not an ideal space to hang for hours with friends. They think of it as a nice brunch spot for the family on Mother's Day—when parents are paying.

Instead, young Swedes around Eklöw's age embrace a different coffee landscape than their parents, flocking to chains proliferating in Stockholm: Wayne's Coffee, Starbucks, and Espresso House. These chains offer ample outlets to plug in and stick around. Coffee drinkers looking for a more relaxed environment head to cozier cafes with niche interests and specialized coffee programs, typically found in younger neighborhoods, like Södermalm.

This is nothing revolutionary. All over the world, teenagers break with tradition and forge their own way, and the coffee culture of a given place at a given time reflects that. But what's telling about this particular shift in Sweden is that it comes at a time when the country's cultural identity is at a crossroads, due to rising issues of immigration and economic well-being. Just as the youth are departing from konditori in droves, they are also openly questioning what it means to be Swedish, and how they intend to shape the country's future for themselves. And they're figuring it all out over fika.

For most of its history, Sweden was a country of conquest. Vikings carried out raids en route to Constantinople and strings of foreign tyrants ruled the land periodically: Swedes were thrust into conflict for centuries on end. Now, the last thing on the minds of young Swedes is war.

In a country that hasn't fought for over 200 years, the youth here look inward, and examine the problems within Sweden's borders. Cafes and coffee shops serve as unofficial think tanks—meeting places where teens can discuss the politics of the day over fika, just as they have for hundreds of years.

Sitting in the back of Vurma Hornstull, a quaint coffee shop in Södermalm, Vanya Isaksson, 18, and Ebba Lindberg, 17, went through a lengthy list of issues with us. "Over the last year, there have been a ton of people [living] on the streets," Lindberg explained. "It all happened very fast—like, they came from nowhere."

Lindberg is referring to the recent Middle Eastern migrant crisis that has knocked on the small country's front door. Since the civil war in Syria unfolded, Sweden, with its wealth of social welfare, welcomed nearly 160,000 refugees in 2015—more than any other European country per capita. The result has been a stark political divide between young and old on how to handle the situation.

Lindberg and Isaksson, along with most of the subjects we spoke with, expressed anger when asked about those who strongly oppose the naturalization of refugees, such as the right-wing Swedish Democrats, who have strengthened their support base amongst older Swedes. "[They're] terrible!" Isaksson responded, almost instinctively, putting down her coffee. "It's a heartbreaking issue," Lindberg added. "And we're pissed off that we can't directly help."

The two young women said their friends volunteer and donate to refugee aid charities when they can. Others have joined rallies, in cities like Stockholm and Malmö, against anti-refugee sentiments.

But for Isaksson, who recently dropped out of high school, finding a job has been her utmost concern. Compared to the EU average, Sweden's youth unemployment has been historically high in recent years, hovering around 19 percent. Not to mention, Stockholm is considered to be one of the most expensive cities in the world, leading to high rates of debt amongst the youth.

"It's hard to find a good job [here] when you're under 18," Isaksson explained, "let alone somewhere you can afford to live."

To remedy this, numerous young Swedes we met at cafes across Stockholm told us that they're looking to move or study elsewhere. However, in order to do so, there are unavoidable realities of emigration—especially for women.

Today, Sweden is widely praised as one of the most progressive nations in the world when it comes to gender equality and feminism. So when young women with whom we spoke mentioned moving to other countries, one of their main concerns was leaving behind that egalitarian spirit. Some resented the idea of being catcalled, while others rolled their eyes at the idea of enduring traditional courtship rituals, such as a man buying them a drink.

While talking to Julia Stenqvist at Cafe Blå Lotus in Södermalm, where she fikas often, the 19-year-old said she wants to relocate to London to study design. But there's a problem: "We assume [school] will be free," Stenqvist said, "Yet, as we get older and look elsewhere, we realize Sweden is not the norm."

For her friend, Trisha Nazmul, 23, a second-generation Swede whose parents immigrated from India, recent talk of the migrant crisis, and the issues of assimilation it raises, has made her revisit her own family's experience. "I still love India," she said to us, "but this is home for me." It's the country where she fikas along with her family and Swedish-born friends.

"There's this idea [here] that either you're Swedish, or you're not. You can't be both," Stenqvist quickly interjected. "But it's not about being one or the other." Therein lies the cultural collision that is raging on in Sweden: who, or what, is Swedish?

Within these debates over feminism and racism, high unemployment and porous borders, there is a growing sense that Swedish society and its values are in flux. Together, they pull at the ideological fabric of the city and country. They call into question what the Scandinavian nation will look like in the coming years. And the city's cafes, serving as cozy refuge from harsh winters and momentous political tides, will bear witness to it all. •

What's In Store

INTERVIEW AND PHOTOGRAPHS
Adam Goldberg and Daniela Velasco

In Stockholm, all coffee roads lead to Johan & Nyström. It began roasting coffee in Stockholm over a decade ago, and still has the pluck that made it the most influential operation in the city. The trailblazing roaster and concept shop introduced Stockholm's cafes, restaurants, and consumers to the idea that coffee didn't have to come from a Nestlé-owned brand or be classified only by dark or light roast. Johan Damgaard, now a central figure on the local scene, has trained and mentored many of the city's best shop owners and new-school roasters. In other words, he's seen it all. He remembers knocking down doors and being laughed at when he first suggested the idea that coffee from different regions tasted differently. Years later, Damgaard is watching the next generation come into its own—and he has a few ideas about how it'll all turn out.

Tell us a little about yourself.
I used to work with a chef at a restaurant six friends and I founded back in 2004. But you don't actually spend a lot of time creating something in restaurants; time is mostly spent cleaning the kitchen. I decided I couldn't do it anymore, and went to school to study marketing and economics.

And then?
I got a job at a coffee roaster on the west coast of Sweden. Back then, in the early 2000s, everyone was promoting brands by the color of the roast. No one said anything about where the coffee came from. There was light, middle-dark, and dark roast; that was it.

Which did you sell?
I was selling middle-dark roast. Back then, people were only talking about how much coffee would sell or how much people would like it. You didn't talk about the actual coffee. Many of those roasters were family-owned and conservative; they had been around for over 100 years.

How did you get involved with Johan & Nyström?
I moved to Stockholm to sell coffee for another company in 2001. I'm from southern Sweden, and my dialect is admittedly a little bit strange. When I came here, I didn't know anyone except my girlfriend—now my wife—and I was knocking on doors asking people to buy coffee. I have a theory people bought from me because I was from the countryside and sounded strange. I think they felt bad for me. At the time, Stockholm was dominated by five industrial roasters. As soon as I realized that the reason people were buying my coffee was because they could relate to me, I knew there was an opportunity.

What did you do?
I called my friends back home in Gothenburg and told them that we should do something with coffee where we tease out the farmers and their stories. We started to plan the roastery. We named it Damgaard and Eckfeldt, which, admittedly, sounds like a law firm. Though I guess we had to be a little traditional because, at the time, we were selling to old ladies. We couldn't have a cool name like "Good Dog Coffee" or something, the way we could now. It wasn't cool yet to drink good coffee.

How did you get it off the ground?
We found two brothers way up north in Haparanda on the border between Sweden and Finland where it's really cold. We needed them to build the facility. At the same time,

the barista community in Sweden was slowly growing. We were part of it: We were judging competitions, and competing. When I competed back in 1999, we thought the best cappuccino foam was fluffy and covered in chocolate. What we saw, though, was that the people who work with coffee are the most important part of the experience. They are the ambassadors of coffee, and people can't begin to understand the coffee without them.

What was it like when you first opened?
We started tracking down cafes and coffee shops one by one to sell the beans we roasted. We were really the only ones at the time who were peddling specialty coffee in Stockholm. We started teaching cafe and restaurant owners that coffee can taste several different ways depending on where it was grown. We taught them about coffee from East Africa, Kenya, Ethiopia, Indonesia, and Brazil. We taught them about the different flavors that different brewing methods could bring out in the beans. It was so much more than just light or dark roast. Imagine if you thought that the only two descriptors in wine were white versus red—and then someone tells you that there are variations among reds. It was like that.

Were you mostly selling wholesale?
Yes, it's always been wholesale. We think of the Johan & Nyström on Södermalm as a concept store. It's where we market and educate. We also serve coffee there, of course, and we have seating, but it exists so that we can communicate with the end consumer, and break down that wholesale wall.

Are the baristas still the ambassadors then?
We send everyone who works here on origin trips. We're about 60 people at the company. We have two guys now in Ethiopia and they came back singing, "Hallelujah!" They got a new perspective on life. We see them as our missionaries; we send them to the origin and then they come back and just spread the word. It costs a lot of money, but it's worth it and it works.

Has the way you brew at the concept store changed over the years?
Espresso beverages have always paid the bills, but I still think the AeroPress brews the cleanest cup of coffee. When we first opened the concept store, we only did AeroPress. But AeroPress requires a lot of labor, so it's getting harder to do as we get more popular. Same thing with the V60 and the siphon. Those methods are becoming more challenging because we have lines of customers who don't want to wait.

Figuring out how to brew coffee faster, and make it more convenient, while retaining quality is really, really hard.

Do you think it's possible?
There are the Blue Bottle guys, who have a lot of equity money coming in, and they're still brewing it by hand. It still takes time. The more time it takes, the more you have to narrow down where you can open up the shop. You can't open up a shop where it takes 10 minutes to get a cup of coffee if you're outside the city. But it works in hectic areas of Stockholm or New York City because cafes are where people go to escape.

Who are your most interesting wholesale clients?
Probably our fine-dining clients. We realized

a little while back that fine dining restaurants served great food and crap coffee. You pay for an expensive dinner and you finish off and think, "Is this it?" At one of our first restaurant meetings, we were laughed at, and told that the last time anyone opened a roastery in Sweden was way back in 1958.

Has that changed over the years?

Now, 10 years later, the landscape is quite competitive. There used to be nine commodity roasters, or "industrial dragons," as I call them. We're not even their competition; we're small by comparison. And then pop, pop, pop the micro-roasters started to popping up like seedlings. We've trained some of them. We don't see them as competitors; the more people who talk about quality, the better it is for us. We want people to

stop drinking the not-so-sustainable machine-picked coffee. Period.

Where do you see Johan & Nyström in a decade?

It's similar to the beer brewing industry. There are some microbreweries that are only good because they're microbreweries. Some of them actually have beer that tastes worse than the big breweries. It's the same thing in coffee. Many people are attracted to the romantic feeling of standing in a garage and roasting coffee in a Merino wool hat with tattoos. I do actually have tattoos, but it's that typical hipster dream, you know? After a year, most of those people realize it's a lot of hard work and not all fun. Right now, we're at 30 to 40 microroasters in Sweden and about 10 in Stockholm. We want to be dedicated to quality, always. •

Bookends

WORDS Elyssa Goldberg
PHOTOGRAPHS Adam Goldberg and Daniela Velasco

In the back room of a dockside boathouse on Djurgården, a Stockholm garden island that's home to sweeping farmland and a mid-century amusement park, dinner service at Oaxen Krog is in full swing. There, chef Magnus Ek and his team fill shallow bowls with roasted cabbage-mushroom broth as they airlift thinly sliced pieces of reindeer to place on top. They squirt a few drops of juniper oil and finish the whole thing with blackberries before sending the dishes out. Several courses later, in the low-lit room, a gooseneck kettle and Chemex arrive to the table. The sommelier begins to describe the coffee beans on offer, a special "Oaxen blend" from Johan & Nyström, with the same gusto as he did Champagne.

In Stockholm, fine-dining restaurants have an unusually strong affinity for coffee, compared to restaurants of the same caliber elsewhere in the world. It's not uncommon for diners at Michelin three-starred restaurants in Paris and New York to finish a meal with pod coffee, the burnt flavor of corporate brews imprinted as their last memory of dinner after plunking down $500 per person.

This is not as often the case in Stockholm, where high-end institutions, from Mathias Dahlgren, Oaxen Krog, and Franzén to Gastrologik and Omakase, trick out their coffee programs with the same attention to detail as they do every other aspect of the experience.

"Don't make any relationships with big companies that mass produce." It was a simple motto that laid the groundwork for the kitchen at Gastrologik, a restaurant in Ostermalm with food as clean and precise as the interior is sleek and modern. But it wasn't easy: the big companies come courting, offering discounts on kitchen products and promising to subsidize tableware if only the restaurant will agree to partner. "Alcohol is the worst. You get calls where a liquor company promises to fund your whole restaurant if you just agree to slap their logo on everything. We didn't want anything to do with that," says Anton Bjuhr, the pastry chef (and resident coffee geek) at Gastrologik.

Nespresso was one of those companies: It offered Gastrologik free machines. But that coffee wasn't in line with the philosophy of the restaurant, which prides itself on working with local producers and the best possible products. So Gastrologik called Johan & Nyström, at the time the best (and now the biggest) micro roaster in Stockholm.

Five years ago, Bjuhr and chef Jacob Holmstrom, co-founders of Gastrologik, didn't know much about coffee, but they knew they had a nice espresso machine and knew they wanted to learn how to use it. "The thing is, in Sweden, we don't drink much espresso. We phoned Johan & Nyström and asked, 'Could you guide us through the world of espresso?'" Stockholm was still at the front end of what the folks at Johan & Nyström told them was a "coffee revolution." The coffee pros made it easy: They mixed a special Gastrologik bean blend and sent someone over to walk the team through cupping and proper brewing techniques using various gadgets.

Bjuhr attributes the desire to have a thoughtful coffee program to tradition. "In Sweden, everyone spends time with family or friends over coffee. You always have fika at the same time every day. It's an important part of the culture," he said. "We do this every single day, after meals too."

Descriptions of aromas and flavors in the coffee made sense to Bjuhr; it was the same language the restaurant used to describe the difference between two types of raspberries or onions. "That's when it got interesting to me," he said.

"Now he drinks more coffee than anyone else here," joked Holmstrom.

A meal at Gastrologik ends with Chemex. And, though they never set out to be a restaurant known for making good coffee, they started winning awards for it. "We just thought that coffee should be as important as anything else in the restaurants—the lamps, the chairs, the cutlery, the fruit, everything," said Holmstrom.

At Franzén, chef Björn Frantzén admits that the reason they started serving Chemex at the restaurant almost a decade ago was because, "We wanted to have the newest and coolest things." If they could play around with molecular gastronomy in the kitchen, the least they could do was get familiar with pour-overs, which made more sense to him than espresso. "It's almost like a consommé of coffee, and most of the bitterness is removed from it."

As with everything else these restaurants do, success depends on a tight-knit group of producers and purveyors committed to high-quality products. Gastrologik, Oaxen Krog, and Franzén all feel indebted to Johan & Nyström in that respect, for making coffee more approachable, and for showing them the ropes.

At newer restaurants such as Omakase, which serves a tasting menu where "every dish has an element of meat somewhere," as sommelier Henrik Heed describes it, a good coffee program was essential. "People in Stockholm are getting more and more into coffee, so finishing off the meal with simple black coffee wasn't really an option," he says.

The restaurant works with Nicaraguan, Ethiopian, and Kenyan beans—which their servers know backwards and forwards, because customers actually ask about them all the time. "Yesterday we had a man who was about 65 years old here with his wife, and he asked me every question imaginable about the coffee. 'Where was it sourced?' 'What is the best way to brew it?'"

Chef Frantzén prefers to serve lighter roasts, even though Swedes traditionally drink darker roasts. "If you think of it like bread, when you put bread in the toaster, you can toast it until it's black and almost charred. But when you taste it, it just tastes like burned bread. It's the same thing with a bean. Lighter roasts give you a better sense of what the bean actually tastes like."

Heed fixates on perfecting coffee service because he knows diners' memories are faulty. "When I ask guests after a meal which dishes they liked best, they almost always say the dishes at the beginning and end of the meal," he says. "It's why you need to choose a good Champagne to start and a great coffee to finish."

Swedes love their coffee. Many drink coffee throughout the day and have built up mighty caffeine tolerances. Frantzén compares that tolerance to something he once witnessed in Spain. In Madrid years ago, he watched road workers drink several glasses of wine with pizza. "If we did that in Sweden, people would think we were alcoholics. But it's the same in Sweden. We drink a lot of coffee—next to Finland, the most per person in the world—it's just what we do. People here expect it."

In the future, at Franzén at least, chefs will be expected to know the coffee program inside and out, the same way they do every food item that leaves the kitchen. Says Frantzén, "If a normal chef can go on and on about coffee—about the bean, the origin, the production, everything—then that's the ultimate restaurant. Everybody should know that nothing ends up at Frantzén by chance." •

Opposite page: Oaxen Krog.

Björn Frantzén, Frantzén.

Jacob Holmstrom and Anton Bjuhr, Gatrologik.

Henrik Heed, Omakase Köttslöjd.

The People's Roaster

INTERVIEW Micha Van Dinther
PHOTOGRAPHS Mikael Axelsson

In Stockholm, the coffee-drinking population can roughly be divided into two camps. On one side there is the specialty coffee crowd that parses the beverage as if it were a fine bottle of Chablis. On the other, there are those who gulp copious amounts of a dark-roasted, tar-like fluid in the same way it has been drunk during *fika* in Swedish households since the early 1900s. Aadel Kersh, a coffee roaster of Finnish-Palestinian descent, wants to close the gap between the two.

To many, he's an outsider espousing an outdated style of Swedish coffee considered by many to be unrefined in flavor. To the rest, he's a local hero. Kersh's operation grew from a tiny start-up in his dad's garage to a tricked out roastery cranking out 25 kilos per batch—all while refusing to bend to the trendy third wave of light roasts flooding the city. We met up with him at his suburban Gustavsberg roaster to talk about his accidental detour into coffee, food elitism, habitual coffee consumption, and why his roasting style is so contentious.

How did you first get started with coffee roasting?
I had no idea about specialty coffee when I first started experimenting with roasting on my stove at home. I'm glad I didn't find out about it until later, because that delay really let me develop my own style of roasting. I did my own thing, with zero outside influences in mind. It was affirming when people around me seemed to like the taste of it.

Looking back, how do you view that early period?
I'm really proud of it all. I think it's important not to listen too much to other people's opinions, because it can be discouraging. Had I known that I needed the machinery that I have today to roast coffee the way I want it, I would never have reached this stage. I only had around 30,000 kronor [approximately 3,500 USD] when I first opened shop—barely enough for raw materials to last a couple of days.

Stockholm is known for having quite a sophisticated third wave coffee scene, especially with respect to filter brews. But you have intentionally chosen to go your own way and stay somewhat out of the local specialty coffee scene. Why?
The market in Sweden is still too small for all the competition out there, and I'm not looking to offer yet another specialty coffee to those who are in the know. Instead, I'd like to reach out to those who love a good cup of coffee, but don't necessarily know a whole lot about what goes into making it. My style of roasting isn't for the nerds—it attracts a different audience.

What kind of audience?
You've got the Swedish style, industrially roasted coffee, which is intensely strong and pitch-black. Then you have specialty coffee, which is often a lighter roast. They are each other's opposites, but just the same. It's like a devout Muslim versus a committed atheist: It's the same type of person, just with opposite convictions. I'm somewhere in between.

Where on the scale exactly?
Pretty much smack in the middle. I want people to recognize what they are drinking. It's what they expect coffee to taste like—dark, bitter, full, and strong— but still slightly different, because the beans I use are better and are on par with contemporary coffee shops. If you served someone who grew up drinking heavily roasted, Swedish-style coffee a beverage that resembles tea, they are bound to feel confused.

The third wave coffee culture has swept over Stockholm, placing the subtleties of flavor, varietals, and growing regions at the core of the quaffable sensation. At the same time, many old-school coffee drinkers can't relate to it.

What's your take on the city's traditional coffee culture?
We have a strong tradition of dark roasts, which in turn always ensures consistent flavor and, to a certain degree, camouflages substandard beans. People still expect coffee to taste the same as it always did. I can't just ignore that or blow it off, even if lighter roasts are all the rage among a small portion of Swedes who go to the newer shops. Telling someone that enjoys dark roasts that their preferred style of coffee is conceived to conceal the defects of beans is bound to offend that person. I do dark roasts, along with lighter ones, made of quality beans. I try to make local coffee for local people.

How did you go from roasting on your stovetop to roasting for retail distribution?
My first roaster could roast around 400 grams. Once I was ready to trade up, I bought a one-kilo roaster for a tiny coffee bar that I opened up in Södermalm. I got in touch with acquaintances at Urban Deli, a grocery store in the neighborhood. They let me place my roaster on the store floor, and I was roasting in the store three days a week. Roasting 400 to 500 kilos of beans in a single kilo machine was nuts but, at the time, I didn't realize just how nuts it was. After that, I sold my flat so that I could buy a 2.5-kilo roaster.

It was too large for Urban Deli, so I got my father to lend me his garage in the suburbs, so I could turn it into a small roastery. One year later, I traded it in for a six-kilo Giesen roaster. A few years after that and I finally have my 25-kilo Joper roaster. It is super-quiet compared to all the other ones I've had. I'm hoping to keep this one for a few years, and am currently working out of my very own space here in Gustavsberg. It has taken me about four years to get here.

What happens now?
Many of my thoughts revolve around that, because I don't only want stores and restaurants to carry my coffee. Looking around the city, there really aren't that many out-and-out coffee bars. Most coffee-serving spots are restaurants or cafes, and the latter are starting to serve alcoholic beverages as well. This amounts to the fact that coffee never really gets to center stage; it has to compete with food. My hope is that Stockholm will get its very own coffee bars, where coffee really is the star of the show.

Why do you think Stockholm lacks the kind of coffee bars you're describing?
It all goes back to Sweden's strong coffee culture. At the end of the day, we always return to our heritage of fika: drip coffee with cinnamon rolls or other baked goods served at home. Sure, once in a while, we'll cheat with a macchiato or cappuccino at a cafe, but we always tend go back to filter-brewed coffee at home. Abroad, in countries that previously haven't had the same strong culture surrounding coffee, I imagine that there is a more pressing drive to go out for coffee.

What is the key to enticing people to get a cup while out and about then?
We need to meet the general public where they are in terms of the types of flavors and roasts they expect, but also add fresh insight to what coffee can be.

Do coffee bars in Stockholm serve coffee to which a majority of Swedes can't relate?
I know I'm running the risk of making enemies, but I sometimes feel that there is a certain degree of elitism in coffee, and gastronomy in general, in Stockholm. Come on, can't we all just relax a little? Either you break away from Swedish coffee heritage completely by doing something entirely different, or you try to find a way into the very heart of it—and that is something I am still working on. •

Side by Side

WORDS Micha Van Dinther
PHOTOGRAPHS Mikael Axelsson
STYLING Josefin Hååg

A number of age-old Nordic fika traditions are being rediscovered by some of Stockholm's most trailblazing baristas, chefs, and coffee roasters. Here are a few you should try.

KAFFEKASK

Kaffekask is a Scandinavian beverage of coffee laced with distilled spirits, usually brännvin—a liquor distilled from potatoes and grains, like vodka or aquavit. The drink first became popular in the early 1800s in southwestern Sweden. Also referred to as kaffehalva (coffee half) for its ratio of equal parts hot coffee and liquor, the cocktail soon spread to all of Scandinavia, and each country has its own variation. Historically, the drink is consumed in a rural setting—as a means to stay warm while chopping wood, for example. (Swedes joke that it must be the reason for many forestry accidents, which is both very funny…and not funny at all.)

The boozy coffee drink is enjoying a tight-lipped revival in a number of Stockholm's specialty coffee bars such as Kafé Esias. Although not explicitly featured on the menu (for fear it would alert the authorities to establishments serving alcohol without liquor licenses), if you request coffee en skvätt sprit—with a splash of alcohol—you'll experience the real old-fashioned Swedish way of drinking coffee.

According to Nordic folklore, bad luck and mental or physical illness afflicted upon those who heard a cuckoo's call during Lent could be remedied only by a tipple for the cuckoo. The translation for that? Gök, short for kaffegök, another name for the classic beverage during springtime.

KAFFEOST

Kaffeost, or coffee cheese, is a squeaky cheese with a texture reminiscent of halloumi that's finding its way onto grocery store shelves and restaurant tables across the city. Although coffee cheese has been enjoyed by the northern Swedes for centuries, it is still new to many Stockholmers. Coffee cheese was traditionally cooked by the women of the Torne River Valley (a northern municipality that spans the border into Finland) ever since the first livestock were introduced to the area in the 14th century.

When consumed, it is most often cut into tiny chunks and placed at the bottom of the cup before being doused in hot coffee. The softened bits, soaked with coffee, are eaten once you get to the bottom of your mug. It might sound like a bizarre pairing, but combining coffee and cheese is unexpectedly familiar, thanks to sweet treats such as tiramisu, coffee cheesecake, and Colombian hot chocolate with queso. The Swedes just bypass the sugar.

Coffee cheese can be difficult to find since it is made in small batches, but Finska butiken in Hötorgshallen food hall always has it in stock. For DIYers, the cheese is fairly easy to make on your stove with the right ingredients: milk, double cream, and rennet (a complex of enzymes that curdles the casein in milk). If you struggle to find reindeer milk or raw colostrum, which are the traditional ingredients, full-fat cow's milk or goat's milk are adequate substitutes.

MASKROSKAFFE

On March 27, 1940, in the middle of World War II, rationing was imposed upon the Swedish people to discourage the use of foreign currency. The importation of coffee beans was severely affected by this restriction, introducing a number of coffee substitutes to the market. The most popular, and the one that's still around today, is maskroskaffe.

A herbal beverage that looks like a muddy mixture of coffee and tea, maskrokaffe is slightly opaque with a deep, roasted flavor, a slight astringency, and a hint of sweetness. Like coffee, it's brewed. However, maskrokaffe is brewed from the roasted and ground roots of the dandelion plant, which, even in the present day, is consumed and extolled as a health booster.

Renée Voltaire, *the* Stockholm health food icon, popular food philosopher, chef, and queen of green, recently added caffeine-free dandelion coffee to her popular line of health foods, bringing it from the bohemian fringe to the mainstream. She touted the digestive and detoxifying properties of the roots of this unpopular weed.

Enjoy maskroskaffe undiluted, the way you would brew coffee, or, as a wartime article in a 1942 issue of the magazine *Husmodern* suggested: "Mélange with as much coffee as one finds oneself can afford, for example ⅓ to ⅔ coffee." ●

Butterfly Effect

WORDS Elyssa Goldberg
PHOTOGRAPHS Daniela Velasco

The most beloved Swedish roaster is not in Stockholm. To get to Koppi, you'll have to drive to the picturesque southern city of Helsingborg, just across a narrow waterway from Denmark. Since the cafe and roaster opened in 2007, it has earned a cult following all over the world. What Koppi does—remember the Kaffe Tonic?—the rest of the international coffee community soon follows.

Even in the dead of Swedish winter, when bitter cold temperatures challenge even die-hard winter folks, Koppi is a delightful retreat. Chalk it up to the floor-to-ceiling windows that give exquisite views of the city's most striking building, Jacob Hansens Hus, and let in every last ray of natural light (even when it's scarce). Or attribute it to Swedish barista champions and co-founders Anne Lunell and Charles Nystrand, whose commitment to sourcing, roasting, and brewing impeccable coffee never wavers.

It was hard for Koppi to break in. Back in 2007, they could count the number of Swedish roasters on one hand, and the small number of potential customers had preconceived notions of what coffee should be. "The coffee tradition in Sweden is very, very old and very, very new," Lunell, ostensibly Sweden's queen of coffee, told us over a delicate V60 brew. "I think we might be the second biggest consumer of coffee per capita, but it's obviously not quality coffee. People in Sweden like their coffee bitter and dark." It's pretty much the opposite of what Koppi serves.

Lunell and Nystrand, who had previously worked in Norway, favored light roasts to bring out the bean's floral and citrus notes. As Lunell remembered it, "That's where we fell in love with coffee, because we found it could be footing for beautiful and sweet flavors, not bitter ones. Coffee didn't have to taste like cardboard." Because they couldn't find the coffee they liked in Sweden, they wanted to source and roast it themselves.

Almost a decade later, Koppi is thriving, thanks in no small part to its devoted regulars. "In the shop, it's 98 percent regulars at any given time. And any new people quickly become regulars," she joked. "It's not just because of trying our coffee for the first time, though. I think it's the whole experience, and our way of communicating what we're doing."

When they first opened, they had a routine. "When someone stepped up to the counter, we'd say, 'Coffee today is from a farm we worked with in Panama and it's organic,'" remembered Lunell. "We presented it that way to every single customer, so they knew what to expect. Sometimes we'd say it 50 times and forget the 51st, and customers would say, 'So, what's the coffee today?' because they were into our way of working."

In this way, they introduced people to the fact that not all coffee is the same. "It was a good way of getting people into specialty coffee in a humble way. You don't have to force information on them," she said. "We started getting comments like, 'Yeah, I liked the coffee you had on yesterday more.'"

In Stockholm, where Koppi sells its beans wholesale, the scene is still young, according to Lunell. "I'm sure a lot of people will be annoyed by me saying that," she hedged. "I mean, it's a pretty city, and there are a lot of interesting things going on, but at the same time, it's kind of isolated. It's not close to anywhere else on that coast." Helsingborg is closer to Copenhagen, which has large-scale international access. And if Koppi is to open a second location, Copenhagen would be the move. It's much closer to Helsingborg, compared to Stockholm, which is a six-hour drive away. Still, she said, "Oslo is still probably the coffee capital."

Yet, with its beans on the ground all over the world, from the U.S. to Japan and Germany, Koppi may well be Scandinavian coffee's most influential export. •

Opposite page:
Anne Lunell, Koppi Coffee Roasters.

The Nordic Roast, Deconstructed

Most Swedish specialty roasters prefer to roast their beans lightly, coaxing out floral, citrus, and bright, fruity qualities that disappear after they've been scorched at high heat for too long. In the industry, it's referred to as a Nordic roast. And Anne Lunell of Sweden's Koppi Coffee Roasters walked us through the process, pausing at one-minute intervals to show us what happens behind the scenes.

07:00   08:00   09:00   9:30 | Nordic   10:00   10:30 | Nordic
                                       Filter   Espresso
                                       Roast   Roast

One For the Road

INTERVIEW Rachel Eva Lim
PHOTOGRAPHS Adam Goldberg

New York and Stockholm operate on completely different wavelengths. New Yorkers dash around frenzied sidewalks clutching takeaway coffee in one hand while they fiddle with cell phones in the other. Across the Atlantic, locals devote hours to lingering over afternoon cups, connecting with friends without batting an eye that they're doing so in the middle of the workweek. Swedish native and New York transplant Lars Åkerlund wants to marry both personalities—and he hopes his Manhattan cafes, called FIKA, will do just that.

The idea dates back to 2001, when a visit to the Big Apple revealed a dearth of satisfactory fika options. Without hesitation, he quit his lucrative property-flipping business in Sweden and plunged headfirst into the New York cafe scene. What began as a single outpost on 58th Street and Central Park South has since ballooned into a 17-store operation with plans for further expansion.

Åkerlund views FIKA as a transcontinental hybrid—born in Sweden and raised in New York, infusing Scandinavian standards with a touch of Manhattan flair. It's a way of acquainting New Yorkers with traditional fika, an idea he's exported from his home country, while providing respite from their hectic lifestyles. Here, Åkerlund waxes poetic about his love for New York, how growing up Swedish nurtured his particular outlook on coffee, and why convincing construction workers to pony up $2 for a cup of joe paved the way for FIKA's success.

What was your relationship with coffee before you got into the business?
Being a Swede means that coffee has an automatic and important place in your life. It's an integral part of socializing in Sweden, so I started drinking and enjoying coffee at an early age. We're also spoiled with having great quality coffee at our fingertips, which has always made me a bit of a coffee snob.

What were you doing before starting FIKA?
I'm a trained chef and spent a few years in the Stockholm restaurant scene. I quickly grew bored of working in the kitchen and became a bit of a serial entrepreneur, starting and running my own businesses in various fields.

How would you describe yourself as an entrepreneur?
I think any entrepreneur has to be a bit of a risk-taker, and I'm certainly no exception. I go with my gut a lot but am also quite thorough. I believe in doing a lot of research prior to entering any new venture. I also don't believe in problems; they are only mental blocks standing in the way of solutions. If you let things or people stop you too easily, you'll never get very far.

What kinds of businesses were you running before you moved to New York?
I was renovating and flipping apartments in Sweden; it's actually how I raised the capital we needed for our first FIKA location. It took me over five years of house-flipping to raise that initial funding, but it turned out to have been a great way to spend my time. It gave me good practice for building the first eight FIKA locations with my own hands.

How did FIKA first come about?
I took my first trip to New York way back in 2001, fell head over heels in love with the city, and knew I had to create a life here. During that trip, I was having a very hard time finding quality coffee and nice cafes where I could sit down, relax, and take in the city. That's when I realized that Swedish fika culture was needed in New York; I made it my mission to introduce it to the city. The present New York coffee scene is huge and great, but back in 2006—which is when I started FIKA—there was a real void.

What about New York lured you in?
It's been said many times, but New York is truly the greatest city in the world as far as I'm concerned. It can be tough, yes, but I find that it's quite fair—you often get back what you put in. I love the diversity, the endless inspiration, and the constant hustle that can be felt day and night. It's good for a restless soul like mine.

New York is a tough place to try to open a food business. How'd it go at first?
Oh, wow, I could give you enough material for a book! There was nothing but challenges initially, but that's part of the fun. I had to figure everything out the hard way and by myself. Just securing the first space was a huge challenge, as no one really understood the type of place I was trying to open. They all assumed I wanted to open a deli. I read through 34,000 ads and physically visited 97 spaces. Luckily, at the 97th space, I met Kate, who was the only landlord who believed in my vision and was willing to take a chance on me. That ended up being our first location on 58th Street by Central Park South. I'm eternally grateful to her for that.

Why do you think FIKA has been so successful?

We offer something unique. There are great espresso bars, chocolate shops, bakeries, and lunch places in the city, but can you name one other brand that offers all those things at once? I also think that New Yorkers love a genuine concept and story; they also appreciate the time and quality we put into our products and our spaces.

You now have 17 stores. Was expansion always part of the plan?

I set out to build a strong New York brand, and I knew I needed a significant physical presence to do so. Finding the right spaces is hard work, and they're often few and far between or can all become available around the same time. With FIKA, we made sure we were ready to strike when the opportunities presented themselves. I know it seems like our growth happened very quickly—and in some ways it did—but the first seven years were really slow and steady. We took our time building each location, testing out the concept, and creating the infrastructure to allow us to grow at a quicker pace without compromising on quality. That's why we felt ready and confident enough to seize the opportunities to expand when they presented themselves.

You initially imported your beans from Sweden. Why did you eventually put an end to that?

We did this in an effort to be as patriotic as possible. However, it became a logistical nightmare and ultimately very hard for us to control the quality of the beans given the complicated transportation procedures. I also really wanted to be able to select my own beans, create my own recipes, and work locally to ensure a fresh, premium product. Our beans are still roasted according to traditional Swedish methods—for a longer time at a lower heat—even if we're not importing them.

How do your bakery and chocolate options contribute to the FIKA experience?

They're essential. Ultimately, at FIKA, we're trying to tell a story. And any good story needs more than one character. We're really working to create an experience and an environment where our guests can create their own perfect fika moment.

What environment were you hoping to create when brainstorming initial designs for FIKA?

I wanted our guests to feel like they were stepping into something different, as we're trying to be a window into the Swedish culture and way of life. I wanted there to be a certain thoughtfulness to the space and we made sure to use as many Swedish design elements as possible in order to create different miniature environments throughout a single location. The whole idea is that you should feel comfortable coming to FIKA at all times and for all purposes, whether it's a quick breakfast, a business lunch, or an afternoon date.

What attracted you to partnering with Johanson Design to provide FIKA's furniture?

It's always been a fun challenge to see just how far we can take our Swedish concept. As Swedish design is so special, it felt natural to extend this to the furniture we selected for our spaces. Johanson Design's products are of exceptional quality and they're one of the few companies that designs and manufactures its entire collection in Sweden.

What value do you think fika plays in one's daily routine?

I think the biggest luxury we can give ourselves is time: Time to relax and time to enjoy. That's exactly what having a fika is all about. It's also about making that moment special by enjoying high quality items instead of something average that you'll end up regretting half an hour later. Best case scenario: It can set a positive tone for how you treat yourself and your other moments for the rest of the day.

What has been some of the best feedback you've gotten from customers?

I will never forget the first few days of being open on 58th Street. We had a group of construction workers come in and ask for coffee. These were classic New Yorkers, just like in the movies. When they learned that a cup of our brewed coffee was $2 they almost walked out right there and then, saying that it was ridiculous to pay more than 90 cents for a cup. I offered them their coffees on the house. The next day, they all returned saying that they now understood what that extra dollar was for. That was a really cool moment for me.

What are some of your favorite cafes to visit in Stockholm?

If I want something a bit more modern, I'll go to Mellqvist in Vasastan. They're always consistent and make one of the best espressos in the city. For something more traditional, I'll visit Tössebageriet in Östermalm. It's old school, high-end, and a true Stockholm institution.

What's next on deck for FIKA?

We have two more key locations opening up in New York. After that, we want to start growing nationally and eventually internationally. We're also looking at having a presence in select airports and firmly believe that FIKA communicates a tradition that will be embraced worldwide. •

Lit

WORDS Elyssa Goldberg
PHOTOGRAPHS Daniela Velasco

The streets of Stockholm glow with the soft warmth that emanates from lamps perched on windowsills all over the city. Even though winter hasn't officially arrived, the sun has already become lazy, appearing late in the morning and retiring by early afternoon. Those lights are as much holiday decoration as they are a necessity. The sun sets at 2 pm.

Swedes embrace winter more readily than most. Each year brings a long, dark, and bleak winter, and each year Swedes get their lamps and candlesticks ready, gather their friends, and ride it out.

They leave their Christmas lights up long after the holiday is over. They adorn their apartments with brass chamber sticks with white tapers that flicker through the night. They mull wine with cardamom, cinnamon, and cloves to make glögg, as it's called in Sweden, that keeps everybody warm (and, okay, a little bit buzzed). They gather around with friends, cuddle under blankets, keep the fire going, and live slowly, the way you have to if you're going to find a way through the unforgivingly dismal and cold season.

The Swedes call the peace and serenity they get from these cozy gatherings and sentiments "mysig." Similar to the Danish hygge or Norwegian koselig, mysig can roughly be translated to "cozy," but its meaning is broader, encompassing everything from crashing on a couch in pajama pants with a loved one to the feeling of seeing a family heirloom during the holidays and savoring fresh-baked kanelbullar and coffee during fika. As Anna Brones writes in her book *Fika*, "The word is derived from *mysa*, which originally meant 'to smile with contentedness' but has come to be used as a verb indicating enjoying, relaxing, and even cuddling." It has as much to do with atmosphere as it does with sentiments, feelings, situations, and people.

It's an integral part of Swedish existence, and even coffee shops in Stockholm respect its significance.

At first glance, Snickerbackan 7, tucked away in a quiet alley near Biblioteksgatan, the posh shopping street in central Östermalm, defies the Swedish concept of mysig. It is cavernous, with vaulted ceilings, white walls, and concrete floors. There aren't any windows, and the underground space glows dimly with neon lights, some candles, and a few desk lamps. The space should read cold, but it may be the coziest place to fika in all of Stockholm.

The way cafe manager Cymon Reid describes it, little touches—low lighting, plush textiles, dark corners—make even the largest of cafes feel as though they're composed of cozy areas with privacy. "Mysig cafes are ones where you can bunch up with friends for several hours, because in the darker months, there is nothing better than finding a nice, cozy place to share a coffee and cake with friends." •

Morning at Sea

WORDS Elyssa Goldberg
PHOTOGRAPHS Adam Goldberg and Daniela Velasco

Even before chef Magnus Ek opened a two Michelin-starred restaurant in Stockholm, he was enamored by the sea. In the 1990s, Ek and his wife Agneta Green helmed their restaurant, Oaxen Skärgårdskrog, from an isolated island in the southern Stockholm archipelago on the island of Oaxen. Accessible only by ferry and overlooking a marshy shoreline, the restaurant all but begged visitors to linger past dessert and hang by the water.

In the bluff just outside floated a hotel boat open to guests, the Prince Van Orangiën, a luxurious vessel from the 1930s lovingly restored by Ek and Green. The boat had belonged to Dutch shipowner Vahali te Gendt, who spared no expense: rosewood and oak paneling, ebony and ivory flourishes, five different types of marble. He lived on the ship as he sailed around the world (presumably in a bespoke smoking jacket) with a dredge fleet. Ek and Green found it listed for sale in an ad online.

Over six decades later, its restoration became the tireless project of Ek and Green, who maintained the old-world opulence with which it was constructed, while adding a few upgrades: reliable heating for the bitter Nordic cold, modern swing-arm lamps, Toto toilets, and L.A. Bruket bathroom products, among them.

When Ek and Green moved Oaxen from the remote island to Djurgården, the Prince Van Orangiën came with it. Now, the stunning hotel boat welcomes guests to one of its seven cabins in the harbor next to Oaxen Krog and Slip, only a 20-minute walk away from central Stockholm.

As much joy as it provides its guests, Ek and Green will forever be its parents—peering at it from the boathouses next door. When Stockholm's temperatures drop, the days grow long, and the boat closes for business, Ek rises early and boards the boat for some early morning calm on the foggy harbor before staff arrives to the restaurants. Alone, when the clouds roll in before dawn, it's just Ek, the boat, peaceful views of Stockholm, and a piping-hot pot of fresh coffee. •

Top 7: Drip Coffee

1. Kafé Esaias
Drottninggatan 102

2. Snickarbacken 7
Snickarbacken 7

3. Kafé Orion
Norrtullsgatan 10

4. Johan & Nyström
Swedenborgsgatan 7

5. Café Pascal
Norrtullsgatan 4

6. Dome of Visions
Valhallavägen 79

7. Drop Coffee
Wollmar Yxkullsgatan 10

Recipe:
The Perfect Iced Coffee

TOOLS:

Chemex
Chemex filter
Scale
Burr grinder

SERVES 2

INGREDIENTS:

33 g fresh coffee beans, ground to medium coarseness (grains should be the size of sea salt)

370 g water, just below boiling point. Bring 500 g of water to a boil (extra water helps maintain temperature), then let stand for 45 seconds.

185 g of ice

TO PREPARE:

0:00	Place Chemex on scale. Tare to 0 g. Add 185 g of ice. Wet Chemex filter with a quick rinse of water. After all water has passed through, place filter into Chemex. Add 33 g freshly ground coffee, and gently shake Chemex to level out the coffee bed. Re-tare scale to 0 g. Slowly pour 60 g of water onto coffee bed, moving in concentric circles, counterclockwise.
0:30	Finish pouring. Wait for coffee to bloom.
0:45	Slowly pour remaining 310 g of water onto coffee bed moving in concentric circles, counterclockwise. Add about 40 g of water at a time. If the level of the coffee bed rises, slow down your pour.
3:45	Finish pouring. Let remaining water pass through filter.
4:00	Serve immediately over ice.

AB Café
Valborgsmässovägen 34,
Stockholm, Sweden

Bagueri Petrus
Swedenborgsgatan 4B,
Stockholm, Sweden

Café Pascal
Norrtullsgatan 4,
Stockholm, Sweden

Chokladkoppen
Stortorget 18,
Stockholm, Sweden

Coffice
Östgötagatan 29C,
Stockholm, Sweden

Dome Of Visions
Valhallavägen 79,
Stockholm, Sweden

Drop Coffee
Wollmar Yxkullsgatan 10,
Stockholm, Sweden

Epicenter
Malmskillnadsgatan 32,
Stockholm, Sweden

Espressino
116 46, Götgatan 11,
Stockholm, Sweden

Espresso House
Kungsgatan 37,
Stockholm, Sweden

Fabrique
Rosenlundsgatan 28,
Stockholm, Sweden

Fika
66 Pearl St,
New York, NY, US

Frantzén
Lilla Nygatan 21,
Stockholm, Sweden

Gastrologik
Artillerigatan 14,
Stockholm, Sweden

Green Rabbit
Tegnérgatan 17,
Stockholm, Sweden

Johan & Nyström Konceptbutik
Swedenborgsgatan 7,
Stockholm, Sweden

Kafé Esaias
Drottninggatan 102,
Stockholm, Sweden

Kafé Orion
Norrtullsgatan 10,
Stockholm, Sweden

Kersh Kafferosteri
Blecktornsgränd 8,
Stockholm, Sweden

Koppi Coffe Roasters
Norra Storgatan 16,
Helsingborg, Sweden

Lanthandelns Espresso
Fredsgatan 12,
Stockholm, Sweden

Mellqvist Kaffebar
Hornsgatan 78,
Stockholm, Sweden

Nejo's Cafe
Sturegatan 38,
Stockholm, Sweden

Oaxen Krog & Slip
Beckholmsvägen 26,
Stockholm, Sweden

Omakase
Yxsmedsgränd 12,
Stockholm, Sweden

Prince Van Orangiën
Beckholmsvägen 26,
Stockholm, Sweden

Sempre Espresso Bar
Jakobsbergsgatan 5,
Stockholm, Sweden

Snickarbacken 7
Snickarbacken 7,
Stockholm, Sweden

Swedish Bakery
5348 N Clark St,
Chicago, IL, US

Vette-Katten
Kungsgatan 55,
Stockholm, Sweden

Wayne's Coffee
Hornsgatan 3,
Stockholm, Sweden

Weinercaféet
Biblioteksgatan 6,
Stockholm, Sweden

**

This list represents coffee shops
visited, referenced, or interviewed on
background for the making of Drift,
Volume 4: Stockholm.

instagram/@driftmag
twitter/@driftny
facebook/driftny